discovering type with teens

discovering type with teens

A Comprehensive Leader's Guide with Materials for Presenting Psychological Type to Young People

Mollie Allen, Claire Hayman, and Kay Abella

Center for Applications of Psychological Type, Inc. · 2815 NW 13th St., Suite 401 · Gainesville, FL 32609 · 1.800.777.2278 · www.capt.org

Published by
Center for Applications of Psychological Type, Inc.
2815 NW 13th Street, Suite 401
Gainesville, FL 32609
352.375.0160
www.capt.org

Allen, Mollie, 1944-
Discovering type with teens: a comprehensive leader's guide with materials for presenting the Myers-Briggs Type Indicator instrument to young people / Mollie Allen, Claire Hayman, and Kay Abella.
     p. cm.
   Includes bibliographical references.
   ISBN 978-0-935652-89-5 (pbk.)
1. Myers-Briggs Type Indicator. 2. Personality tests for youth. 3. Youth--Psychological testing. I. Hayman, Claire, 1946- II. Abella, Kay
Tytler. III. Title.
   BF698.8.M94A45 2009
   155.5'1828--dc22

                         2009037917

ISBN 13: 978-0-935652-89-5

dedication

Martha Wilson Alcock (1954–2005) shared her comments with
enthusiasm. Her contributions enriched this work and the field of psychological
type. We miss her sunny disposition and practical research.

table of contents

Section 4 Unit-by-Unit Presentation 65

Part III **Extras**

Section 5 Options and Additional Materials 143

Part IV **Resources & Bibliography**

Section 6 List and Script for Reproducible Materials 171

Section 7 Resources 181

important notice

The materials on the CD-ROM included in this book are available for reproduction by facilitators. Please note that these materials are nonetheless copyrighted and may not be used for any other purposes than delivering this program. For specific copyright information, please see the copyright and trademark page.

editor's note

Editor's note to educators and facilitators: The editors and authors of this work have made the progressive decision to support the re-introduction of the historical use of "their" as a gender neutral, *singular* pronoun. This provides continuity in the narrative, relates to the way in which teens (and others) actually speak, and removes the political incorrectness of "his" and the awkwardness of "his or hers." Please note that this construction was a fixture in the English language until, some scholars believe, Latin-based rules of grammar were incorrectly imposed on the rules of English grammar.

preface

THIS BOOK IS THE result of more than fifteen years of introducing the Myers Briggs Type Indicator® (MBTI®) instrument and the ideas behind it, to teenagers in workshop settings, following the administration and scoring of the MBTI instrument.

Most of the activities described in this program were used with gatherings of students, youth leaders, or social youth groups, and they took place in schools, church halls, or camps. Many of them are appropriate for use with individual teens.

In some groups, the ideas of Myers and Briggs were offered as a way for teenagers to understand personality differences. Many teens learned about the MBTI instrument in a humanities class where Myers-Briggs® theory was offered as part of the curriculum under topics such as the study of knowledge and knowing, (epistemology) and the study of self. Other teens learned about the instrument in psychology workshops. Although most workshops took place in one session, the same activities offered at schools covered two blocks, or four periods, over two to four days. Some of the activities have been used one-on-one with individual teens who were exploring career and college options or learning, writing, and homework styles.

Most of the activities were designed for teens in grades nine through twelve. All took place in New Hampshire and Massachusetts and most of the teens were Caucasian Americans.

Readers who work with multicultural youth should consult the work of Daniel Robinson, Pat Battle, Mary Todd, and others who have explored type and multicultural issues. Articles by these and other authors can be found in education conference proceedings available through the Center for Applications of Psychological Type (CAPT®) and in the *Journal of Psychological Type*.

Readers working with at-risk students or students with learning disabilities should consider adapting the program to better serve the needs of those students. Some suggested adaptations are outlined in section 5.

This book is an overview of our experiences in applying the MBTI instrument. It is not intended to replace the *MBTI® Manual* or the necessary training needed to administer and interpret the MBTI results. It does not suggest what settings, groups, individuals, and purposes are appropriate for use of the MBTI instrument. Anyone using the MBTI instrument should read and refer to the manual and attend certification programs to learn about the requirements of administration, interpretation, and proper application of the MBTI instrument.

Case studies presented in this book are composites. Some material is based on student comments that have been edited or modified. Student names have been changed and, when necessary, permission to use the material has been obtained.

acknowledgements

WE WOULD LIKE TO acknowledge many people for their support in completing our work. Margaret Fields and Kyla Alper-Ernst shared their words. Carolyn Mamchur and Kris Geiger shared their work. Theresa Clary searched. Mea Allen and Eileen Clary gave suggestions and encouragement, keeping our interest and motivation alive. Christine St. Jean, Doris Dennehy, Ann Warnock, Kathy Kaditz, Dr. Matt King, Beth Weinberg, and Dee Gould invited us into their classrooms. Dr. Gloria Coulter and Maureen Tisei included this workshop in a high school guidance program. We are especially grateful to hundreds of young people who trusted us as they learned about themselves through the MBTI® instrument. We are especially grateful to the many people at CAPT who supported and helped us along the way including Betsy Styron, CEO; Jamie Johnson, research librarian; Naima Cortes, project manager; Eleanor K. Sommer, editor; designers John Amerson and Gina Smith; and former CAPT editors Keven Ward and Jean Reid.

A million thanks to Anna Aramini, Gail Ellison, Diane Ferris, Bill Jenkins, and Loretta Symons for their dedication in field testing the program. Martha Alcock, Len Tallevi, and Gordon and Carolyn Lawrence were brave enough to slog through the new teen type descriptions and give us their reactions and suggestions.

A special acknowledgement to Leann and Howard who showed us the threshold and to Alicia, Jamie, Jeffrey, Jennifer, Matthew, and Mea who keep the door open.

A special note of gratitude goes to Katharine Myers. She gave gifts of time, encouragement and enthusiasm as the work progressed, and she composed the story of the MBTI development and Isabel Myers in a way that would interest young people.

Finally, special thanks to Kay Abella, our co-author and editor, whose talents not only pulled it all together but also enriched each section.

In the world of type, ideas and exercises, analogies and metaphors are constantly swirling about. If we have inadvertently used any of these without proper acknowledgement, we sincerely regret it.

PART ONE

getting started

introduction

HOW MANY OF US, introduced to the Myers-Briggs Type Indicator® (MBTI®) instrument as adults, have said, "I only wish I had known this sooner?" We have had the privilege of exposing young people to the affirming theories of Jung, Briggs, and Myers. To see students eagerly awaiting their type profiles after the experiential exercises makes all the careful preparation enormously gratifying. Some wanted their own type t-shirts, some wrote humorous skits on various "teacher types," and others had their career horizons expanded. We have heard comments such as these: "You mean adults with my preferences can be pilots?" and "I am really different from most kids in this class. Maybe it means I will be a different kind of math teacher."

Young people are more able to cope with challenging relationships using their MBTI perspective: "I give Tim more time to think things out since I know he has preferences for Introversion" and "My father is my total opposite!" Years after one of our classroom sessions, one student remarked, "I don't remember my 'letters' but I'm always ready to hear that there is another way to look at things. I know everyone is not just like me." Type influences teachers too. One teacher eliminated oral participation as a grading requirement in spontaneous, large group discussion. These represent a few of the benefits and rewards that can be experienced when bringing the MBTI instrument into the lives of young people.

When we met each other at the Association for Psychological Type (APT IX) conference in 1991, we had no idea it was the beginning of a collaboration that would end in a book. Since then we have continued raising our children and shared our many experiences introducing type to teens, teachers, and parents. Though our work often takes us outside of type settings, our work with type is always with us.

Mollie works with elementary, middle school and high school students as a special education teacher and uses the MBTI instrument with individuals and groups of young people, parents, mothers, and teachers. She has a bachelor of arts in child development and special education and a master of education in administration and supervision.

Claire, a former social studies teacher of grades six through twelve and museum educator, currently works as an urban high school guidance counselor. She uses the MBTI instrument with education, business, and families. She has a bachelor of arts in history and a master of education in counseling.

Kay had worked many years as an organizational consultant before deciding to focus on the use of psychological type in all areas of life. She founded and edited for seven years *TypeWorks*, a newsletter for professionals using psychological type in their work. She has one daughter.

At the time we began working on this book, there was an increasing emphasis on type dynamics and the functions of the attitudes in type literature and programs. We chose to stay with the four basic dichotomies for two reasons. First, most of our work had been done using the four pairs, and we knew this approach worked. We wanted to share work that had been tested. Teens had benefited so much in particular from knowing about the E–I and J–P attitudes alone that we didn't want to lose that benefit. Second, many Jungian learning style theories are based on the Myers-Briggs dichotomies, and we feared this connection would be less clear if we introduced the concepts of each function in both its introverted and extraverted form.

We've compiled our experiences and thoughts on how adolescence in general and type development theory in particular relate to young people. We hope this emphasis combined with the activities and visuals help you offer fun, lively presentations to teens.

how to use this book

Discovering Type with Teens is a complete resource for introducing the Myers-Briggs Type Indicator® assessment and personality type theory to teens.

Part I provides background information: why type is helpful to teens, issues to consider in using type with teens, and how to get support for and set up a session with teens.

Part II provides everything you need to present a four-hour program to introduce type to teens. We have outlined the preparation process and the step-by-step process to follow, including timing and helpful tips.

Part III offers facilitators alternate and additional exercises and also details ways to adapt the program for special situations.

Part IV contains a list of the reproducible masters and a script for the visual presentation, information about how to submit research data to the Center for Applications of Psychological Type, ethical guidelines for using the MBTI instrument, contact resources, and a bibliography.

Throughout the unit-by-unit presentation, you will note icons that make it easier for you to anticipate the next actions in the program. The key for these icons is on page 67.

In *Discovering Type with Teens*, we introduce four innovative new resources:

1. The worksheet *First Guess Type* (PM-1) is designed especially for teens to self-assess their preferences in each pair.

2. The worksheet *Who Influences You?* (PM-2) allows teens to examine the people in their environments who might influence them to express one preference or the other, thus creating pressure to "falsify" their type. This can create groundbreaking awareness of how type plays out in their current lives.

3. Energetic new illustrations that bring the preferences to life for teens, accompanied by preference descriptors in easily understood language.

4. Descriptions of the sixteen types that are written for teens in everyday language and related to teen settings and issues.

You will notice that the pace of the program is sometimes very different from adult feedback workshops. In testing the program, we consistently found that teens tune out unless activities move quickly, are presented in language they relate to, and allow them to move around and participate frequently. We have designed the program accordingly.

All of these features have been tested with teens and with adults who work with teens and have been shown effective for ages thirteen through twenty. Because all the materials that a facilitator needs are included, the program can be presented multiple times at a reasonable cost.

You may find yourself challenged to quicken the tempo, cut to the chase, and loosen up your style when you work with teens. We guarantee it will pay off!

Making It Easy

We have designed *Discovering Type with Teens* to support you through every stage of using type with teens including the following:

- Deciding if a given application is right and helping you convince the sponsors to give their approval. (See "Why Use Type with Teens" in section 1, page 9, for ideas.)

- Understanding how using type with this population is different and how to anticipate pitfalls you may encounter.

- Setting expectations and overcoming resistance in administering the instrument to a teen group.

- Preparing the student materials, including a report form designed for teens. All you need to add is MBTI instrument.

- Presenting the program with efficient preparation, since all the steps are established and spelled out.

- Using effective innovative visuals, which are provided on an accompanying CD-ROM.

- Allowing you to adapt the program with suggestions for special exercises, timing, and modifications for at-risk youth.

Your Part

Although this ready-to-go program provides everything you need to deliver a type seminar to teens, you must also have some background and knowledge about type and type dynamics in addition to setting aside some time to follow up with students or faculty when needed.

Your Knowledge

Discovering Type with Teens assumes that your own knowledge of type is solid. Knowledge of type dynamics, type development, and ethics of type will serve you well as you use the materials in this program. If you are eligible by virtue of your education to administer the MBTI instrument and have not attended an MBTI® Certification Program, we urge you to consult additional resources to deepen and refresh your expertise, including review of the most current *MBTI® Manual* and books such as *Building People, Building Programs: A Practitioner's Guide for Introducing the MBTI® to Individuals and Organizations* (Lawrence and Martin 2001), which provides a review of MBTI basics and tips for delivering type to groups, including ethical considerations.

Understanding Teen Development

We also suggest that you examine how type fits with where teens are in their lives. Teen years and midlife are two of the trickiest times in life. Teens are buffeted by messages about how they are *supposed* to be, how they *want* to be, and how they *actually are* at the moment.

Type tells them to listen to their own voices. But it must also recognize the pressures on each individual from society, family, and friends. Some teens may not be ready to claim one preference over another, to settle on one type. They may feel like they are being put in a box. They may not want to admit what they prefer or wish they preferred.

In terms of type development, the chief task for teens involved in this program is to discover and learn to use their preferred approaches well. Finding out "who they are" at the moment provides a solid foundation for maturation. In later years, they will learn to use their less-preferred approaches. The other message of this program is that everyone is eventually capable of using both preferences. The facilitator needs to balance these two messages: You CAN use both preferences, but you don't have to do it right now.

We do not want to create more stress in teens. The facilitator's job is to assure them that they do not need to feel pressured to make decisions; there is no box they have to fit into. All they need to do is open their minds and think about the issues. The rest will follow because defining one's self is a lifelong task.

Follow-up

Finally, we urge you to make this introduction only the *beginning* of your work with type and teens. In section 1 (see "Increasing the Payoff," page 26) we suggest a number of ways to reinforce and deepen the use of type by teens. Think of this introductory session as opening a door. Take every opportunity to help teens explore beyond the door, applying type to such issues as study skills, choosing a college, exploring extracurricular activities, and handling issues with family and friends.

1

how type works with teens

1

how type works with teens

Why Use Type with Teens?

Knowledge of psychological type is helpful and enriching to people of any age. It can, however, have a special influence on the lives of teens, given the pressures they face and their social and developmental needs. Here are some of the ways MBTI feedback and type theory can positively influence teens. Obviously, the effect on each student depends on their individual experiences and on the degree of follow-through and application of type concepts in their environments.

Identity

- Teens are sensitive to differences in people and usually try to establish their own identity. Type helps teens view their own strengths and struggles realistically. It gives a positive language for describing and making sense of the ways they like to take in information, make decisions, and interact with the world. Teens often react to type with "Now I understand! I'm OK the way I am." Type helps foster a positive self-concept without diminishing any other type or person.

Connecting

- Teenagers are reaching out to build substantive relationships with other people. Type can explain why they build relationships so easily with some people and just don't connect with others.

- Students learn to be less judgmental about the lifestyles of other people, realizing that what is boring, irrelevant, or interesting to them may not be so for others. Presenting opinions with attitudes, such as "This movie was too sentimental *for me*" or "Mr. Smith's English class is so boring *to me*" helps teens develop open minds and nonjudgmental relationships.

Having good relationships with my teachers and the other students is very important to me.

Feeling Different

- Some teens feel different; others feel confused or isolated. Many feel pressured to be as others want them to be. Type delivers the message that differences are OK and that each type has inherent strengths and value.

Tolerance

- Young people tend to see things in black and white, leading them to jump to conclusions about the behavior of others or categorize people by social groups, etc. The silent peer is a "snob." An outgoing student is an "airhead." Type places these behaviors in a continuum of normal and helps a teenager understand the preferences behind some behaviors.

- Struggling to define their own views, teenagers often reject or accept the views of other people unconditionally. Type invites them to see these views as different from their own but not necessarily right or wrong.

Living with Rules

- Type introduces the idea that a rule or law that a teen might find stupid or unfair may make perfect sense from another point of view, that is, to someone with different type preferences. Type invites teenagers to look at the preferences behind the rule.

Family Life

- Type helps teenagers understand stresses and conflict at home, whether between parents, between parents and children, or between siblings. Teenagers who are different in type from other family members find validation for their minority approach and recognize that all types bring value to the family. If family members also learn about type, they learn to respect the strengths of types in the family. Teens can become more accepting of differences even if they can't understand them. Teens learn to view family decisions as a choice between differing preferences, not win-lose situations in which decisions are forced on them.

Separating from Parents

- A big issue for teenagers is the drive to become independent from their parents, often by rejecting everything the parents do and say. Type can help teenagers see differences in positive terms and offers understanding instead of criticism.

  Maybe Mom wants to hear about my day because she prefers Extraversion, not because she wants to spy. Dad frets about my plans changing because he has a preference for Judging and likes things to be settled. I may not agree with them, but their behavior does make sense, given their preferences.

Planning the Future

- In looking toward career or college, young people feel enormous pressure to decide what is important to them and what they want to do with their lives. Type often decreases the pressure by validating many approaches, including putting off the decision, rejecting the idea of college, or looking at many options before deciding.

- In thinking about the future, type helps teenagers think about their experiences and reactions in life so far and draw some conclusions about what kind of career or education might fit them best. When students participate in a job shadowing or mentor program, they may even come across the MBTI instrument in the workplace.

The College Search

- When looking at colleges, type can help teenagers understand why they approach the process as they do, from planning visits and gathering information to making the final decisions. Type gives students language for explaining their approaches, especially when such approaches differ from those of parents or advisors.

Decision Making

- Teens are often in the process of learning to use critical thinking in decision making. The four pairs of preferences, along with the Zig-Zag model (see page 26), can be used for making big decisions such as choosing a college and also for less consequential decisions such as decisions about extracurricular activities or what classes to take. The Zig-Zag model uses type concepts specifically to guide a teen through a structured path examining facts, possibilities, logic, and personal values. In this way, teens learn to consider all factors, not just those to which their preferences pull them. When the final decision is made, type makes it easier for a student to explain the reasons for the choice to others. This can be especially helpful in making major decisions such as which college to attend.

Academics

- Type can shed light on why a student may enjoy or do well in some classrooms or structures and not in others. Less successful experiences may be related to less developed preferences or less-preferred preferences. Knowledge of type may help students understand that they sometimes have to work *against* their preferences, having to work harder in some areas than others. For example, a student having trouble with math may learn to view that difficulty as the flip side of preferences that make him comfortable with creative writing. The student still has to take math but at least gains a new perspective about his preferences and may be encouraged to develop the less-preferred preferences.

Understanding Teachers

- Type encourages tolerance of differences between teachers. Why does one teacher mark down because there is no title page and another not care about such details? Why does one teacher change the due date when another sticks to the original date? Students may come to understand some of these differences as type based, not as unfair behavior designed to confuse or irritate the student. When students can relate assignments and testing and evaluations to possible teachers' preferences, they may be able to communicate better with a given teacher and anticipate questions and assignments.

Asking for Help

- A student who understands type can explain why he or she needs help and accept that need as justified. The student can approach the teacher for help in a way that considers the preferences of the teacher, but also makes clear the needs of the student.

Understanding Classroom Behavior

- Type can help teenagers understand differences in class behavior. They begin to see why oral participation is natural for some students and not for others, and why some students pay great attention to details and facts while others seem to stray far from the topic. With this information, students can then place their own behaviors in this continuum of the normal.

Managing Homework

- Type knowledge can help teenagers develop a system for homework that works for them. Then, instead of rejecting advice out of hand, the student can use type to explain to parents and teachers why a different approach works best for him or her.

Working in Teams

- Teenagers work increasingly in teams, not just in sports, but for class projects, student government, and outside activities. Type often helps them accept that team members will naturally work in different ways, view deadlines and commitments differently, and communicate in various ways. Another team member may come up with just as good a product but by working in very different ways. Type teaches that a team with a range of different types may end up with a more effective output. Teens see how to integrate their approaches with those of other types and, when necessary, call on less-preferred functions.

Dating

- In dating, a teen often attributes attraction, rejection, or conflict to innate faults—his or her own or the other person's. Type helps teens validate partners and see differences as valid rather than fatal flaws. Because it enhances a person's self-esteem, type can help teenagers to resist a partner's attempt to manipulate them or put them down.

Looking at Psychology

- Type introduces psychological issues in a nonpathological way. It presents conflict and challenges between people as differences of preference, not mental or personality problems.

Looking at Tests

- Teenagers are strongly affected by standardized tests that claim to measure personality characteristics precisely; beliefs about heredity, which can't be changed; or deficits which must be "fixed." By contrast, MBTI results encourage teens to reject or question the results. They are given a proactive tool to observe themselves and manage their behavior. Type is something that is positive with which they can work.

Special Issues for Using Type with Teens

We all know that teens learn in some ways like adults, and in many ways *not* like adults. The following suggestions are methods that have worked for us in adapting the learning experience of psychological type to the needs of teens.

- All learners enjoy a change of pace, but we find it essential in working with teenagers. In working with young people, you will want to provide more varied activities than you would for an adult audience. Keep teens alert by getting them out of their seats and allow for lots of group interaction. Give frequent breaks.

  Try changing the arrangement of the room for different parts of the program. Have students stand to observe an activity. Use props students can play with, such as Koosh balls or small stuffed animals. Sometimes we have them pass this prop on to whoever is talking. Add any other props that might be fun and keep the group involved. Basically we have found that to keep teens' attention, you need to do the unexpected, keep the pace fast, and avoid belaboring points.

- Do some research about teens and type development in general. There is more than one idea on type development. Keep in mind that the development of the four mental functions can vary throughout a person's life. This may influence the reported results and observed behavior of teens. In addition, ages and development may affect how reliably teens respond to the MBTI instrument (see the *MBTI® Manual* pages 27–33 for discussion on type development, and pages 161–162 for a discussion on reliability of age groups).

Learning about my personality type has helped me make better use of my study time.

- We recommend groups of 12 to 25 for presenting this type of feedback to young people. We discourage a group of more than 25. Increasing the group size forces trade-offs. Some teens can be quite opinionated, even if wrong, in how they interpret their MBTI results and the conclusions they draw. If the group gets too big, opportunities to respond to inaccuracies and stereotyping are lost. Teens are often reluctant to test their understanding or ask questions. A smaller audience allows the facilitator to read body language and to notice when someone is getting lost. At the same time, if the group is too small, there will be less type diversity to draw on.

fyi

During early use of this program, we presented to very large groups (up to 75 students) as we had seen done at an APTi conference. Even though the Myers-Briggs workshop was rated as the most favorite activity by almost all of the students at the end of the school year, such large groups did not allow for questions or conversations that demonstrate thorough understanding of this powerful instrument. We discontinued this kind of presentation.

- Teenagers live in a world where "the written document is always right," especially with any kind of test. They are all too willing to see things in black and white, either/or. To counter this, remind them frequently of the possibility of either/or and both. The handwriting metaphor and a symbol such as the yin-yang are good illustrations to emphasize the either/or nature of the preferences. Keep this kind of visual aid prominent throughout the session.

- To discourage the black-and-white approach, use verbs rather than nouns in talking about preferences. For example, "When I am extraverting I . . ." versus "I am an Extravert" or "I have preferences for ENFJ" versus "I am an ENFJ."

- Underscore that self-knowledge is more important than the "paper results." Do this by giving the teens a chance to self-assess themselves on each set of preferences. Emphasize that their reactions in the session are just as valid as their answers on the instrument. When you speak one-on-one, give weight to each student's self-assessment. Given our extraverted society and their experiences with most assessments, many teens are all too willing to give up their self-assessment if it is different from results on paper.

- It is possible to introduce type ideas without using the MBTI instrument. You can use the cartoons and descriptions in this program and simply allow the teen participants to self-select each preference. They can still use the full type descriptions to check their self-selections. For a discussion of the pros and cons of using the Indicator and further directions for presenting type without feedback, see "Options and Additional Materials" in section 5.

- Avoid sarcasm or put-downs about any type, even in jest. Teens are quick to pick up and use negative humor if it is modeled.

- It is critical to demonstrate to young people how each preference pair shows up in their everyday life; otherwise personality type remains a dry theory. In the program, we do this by asking students, after they hear about each preference pair, where they see those preferences in their everyday lives. As time allows, we encourage students to share situations in which they think type might be involved and work with others to identify how type understanding might help. If you know enough about the group, you can even bring up problematic circumstances in their lives and how type might help explain or improve the situation.

  During the program, we point out the following links between preferences and teenagers lives:

  ▸ Understanding E–I differences helps clarify different social-life needs and encourages each student to balance social life and solitude to meet his or her own needs.

  ▸ J–P helps clarify differences in completing tasks and planning social life.

  ▸ S–N is helpful in examining learning styles, teaching styles, and how differences in the two can be managed using type understanding. Teens can see teacher questions, student responses, and test expectations in a new way.

  ▸ T–F can shed light on values and how bad moods can be created when teens see each other as either insensitive or illogical in drawing conclusions.

- Teens tend to be very sensitive about privacy, especially from adults. Model confidentiality. Pass out the results in a way that allows privacy. When you make a group type table to display at the workshop, put an X rather than a name for each individual in the appropriate cell. Privacy is less of an issue when the teens in the group know each other.

fyi

Putting the individual results in separate envelopes with each young person's name on it is time well spent. It reinforces confidentiality, which is part of the ethical use of the Indicator. It also addresses the issue of privacy important to some young people.

- The dynamic will differ when the teens already know each other. They may be more distracted by "what's going on" with them and between them. On the positive side, they will be more likely to open up and more willing to get involved in activities when working with others they know.

- Encourage teens to explore; remind them that self-knowledge and study are life long pursuits. State explicitly: "You decide your preferences. The results from the MBTI instrument are only part of the puzzle." Allow them to argue with or refuse the paper results and to respect their own self-assessment. Allow participants to observe and "pass" on activities or decisions regarding their types. Allow them not to share their self-assessment or MBTI results.

- Type knowledge can be very helpful in understanding and managing conflict in a group of teens. However, we would recommend this application only if you are experienced in the use of the MBTI instrument and in the theories and applications for dealing with conflict.

- Teens often state opinions as facts. Urge them to give examples that include settings and situations. Have plenty of stories and examples that make your point so they'll know what you are looking for.

Questions Teens Frequently Ask About Type

> **Note: In answering questions asked during a session, the key is not to present yourself as the expert. Instead, focus on what concern or doubt might be behind the question and then share information as an equal.**

Is it OK to be in the middle—not to be sure if I'm T or F or J or P?

Being "in the middle" simply means that you do not consistently choose one or the other preference in a pair. At your age, you may still be experimenting with the preferences. Over time, as you think about type and observe yourself, you will probably find that one preference is more like you.

What made me become E or I or S or N?

Many people believe that type is inborn but not inherited. Your preferences have no relationship to your parents or siblings. However, the family you are raised in can make a difference in how you express type preferences. Sometimes family members try to "fix" people who are not like them. Perhaps there is only one person in a family with a preference for Perceiving. Instead of hearing from the family that he or she "brings the joy of fun to our home" and "loving surprises," the child may only hear jokes and negative comments about "playing around instead of doing a good job" or being "irresponsible." The child may go against his or her own type to try to fit in. Growing up this way, may make finding true preferences difficult, and it can take a long time.

There is ongoing research into how personality preferences relate to physical and mental processes. For instance research by Martha Alcock, Ph.D., revealed actual differences in the brain activity of those who prefer Extraversion and Introversion as they learn. Further research is being done to see how other preferences may be reflected in a person's physical makeup.

What if I think the description of my type is wrong?

Only you can decide what type fits you best. If the result of the Indicator, or the opinion of someone else, does not feel right, then you should feel free to ignore it. You can give some thought to why you might appear to be the other type, but the final decision is yours.

Will my type preferences change as I get older?

Type preferences remain consistent throughout life, even though there may be times when you are not able to act as you prefer or you may respond differently to the MBTI instrument. For example, a person may prefer Perceiving but may come from a very structured family so that she needs to act as though she prefers Judging. But, when she is free to choose later in life, she would probably begin to act more in accordance with her preference for Perceiving.

How can my parents find out about type? What if my parents think my type is different from what I think it is?

Your parents, or anyone else, can attend a workshop on type. Or they can learn about their types from a practitioner trained to administer and interpret the MBTI instrument. Such practitioners are most easily found at local colleges, community centers, or churches or temples. If they prefer, your parents can simply do some reading about type. (Facilitators can offer the names of some books they feel are reliable.) Your parents might consult the Web site of the Myers & Briggs Foundation, a not-for-profit educational organization that provides accurate and reliable information about type: www.myersbriggs.org.

Once your parents learn about type, they should realize that they cannot tell you what type you are. Only you can decide. Sometimes discussing type as a family is a wonderful way to learn about how members view the world differently.

Can't I just guess my parents' type? My boyfriend's? My teacher's?

Guessing other someone else's type is a bad idea. First, it suggests that you know them better than they know themselves. Second, you will be working only from observation of behavior and speech. Preferences are internal and cannot be seen from the outside. A person's behavior or speech is affected by many things besides preferences.

What you can do is make some educated guesses about what a person may prefer and use that to understand them better. But do not make a firm decision and then tell them what type they are or treat them accordingly. You may be wrong.

Since I am an Introvert, why do I get graded on how much I participate?

Type is about what you *prefer*. Though you may prefer not to participate orally, you still need to meet the expectations of others when they are in charge or when they have valid reasons for their requirements. Knowing about your type may help you talk to your teachers about how you learn best and how they can help you be prepared for class discussions where you may be marked on participation.

How Type Works with Teens

Should people of different types date each other?

People of different types can relate in many different ways. The important thing is to use your understanding of type to understand and accept differences between you. Knowing about your type and that of the person you are dating may allow you to communicate better and to handle conflict more smoothly.

I am very F at home but very T when I am out with my friends. Which am I?

Chances are that, either at home or with your friends, some other influence is working on you to make you act in a way different from your preference. For example, maybe your friends have a very objective fact-oriented approach and you naturally go along with that. But at home where you feel comfortable being more subjective and value oriented, you stick to your Feeling preference. Or maybe it is just the opposite.

If there are about an equal number of Js and Ps, why does everyone talk about how important it is to be on time?

A culture often reinforces certain preferences over others. Many people find that modern western culture emphasizes planning and structure, so the Judging preference seems more accepted. You need to be aware of these pressures, and recognize that sometimes you may need to change your behavior to accommodate cultural norms. But it doesn't mean your type is wrong.

Are popular kids always ones who prefer Extraversion?

It may seem that way because Extraverted types, more than Introverted types, are often more outgoing and more likely to reach out to others and engage with the outside world. But the concept of "popularity" is an elusive one. If you mean being liked by others, then you need to know that all types find people they enjoy being with and who enjoy them. Having more friends is not necessarily better than having a few friends. It is the quality of relationships that matters. People who learn about type and use it to understand others may find themselves comfortable with a wider range of people.

Which type is most creative?

The Sensing–Intuition pair is most often associated with creativity. People of both preferences are creative, but in different ways. People with a preference for Sensing most often use their creativity to create new versions of established things, enhancing what is there. People with a preference for Intuition, on the other hand, are more likely to use their creativity to do something completely new. People who prefer Sensing and people who prefer Intuition are both found in creative careers and the arts.

Is type related to birth order? Is type inherited?

There is no evidence that type is related to either birth order or heredity.

What type do you think the president of the U. S. (or some other famous person) is?

It is impossible to get accurate clues to the type of a famous person because they are acted on by so many strong influences besides type, and the information we get about them is filtered by the media or their own image makers. It is more helpful to understand yourself and how to use type knowledge than to try to guess other people's types. If you do want to practice finding clues to a person's type, it is probably better to do it on characters from literature or movies.

Who wrote the questions on the MBTI instrument?

Katherine Briggs and Isabel Briggs Myers designed the original questions. Isabel refined them through the 1960s. The MBTI instrument was recently re-edited and many of the original questions were retained. Some of the wording of questions was updated.

Do people get along better with people of similar type than with people of the opposite type?

Not necessarily. For example, two EJ types may want to be in charge and may get into conflict about who will be the leader. Or two people with Feeling preferences may base their decisions on two different value systems and not be able to compromise. In actuality, many things influence who you are and who you get along with—things like common interests, values, or backgrounds. Type may help us to understand and manage conflict but it may not always eliminate it.

Why don't we just share our types with (the class) everyone right now?

The information is new to everyone and some people may want to question and reflect on it before they share with others. MBTI results may or not be accurate and more time for exploration may be helpful for everyone. If I assume that everyone wants to share new information right away, I may have a bias toward Extraversion preference and may unintentionally put pressure on others to operate this way too. Individuals may share their types in their own way and time.

Looking at type distributions over career choices, my type doesn't seem to choose engineering but that is what I hope to study. What does this mean?

Every career field is open to every type. Sometimes certain types choose a field more than others but that does not mean you should eliminate a choice because fewer of your type choose it. Keep in mind that type is only one small piece of what to consider when choosing a major or a career. You will want to take a look at your academic and life interests, talents, values, and goals in addition to your type.

Sometimes a type less represented in a certain field may bring a much needed perspective. Knowing that you may be in the minority can help you anticipate your reaction to working in that field and prepare you to find support and strategies for success.

Note: If your group shows a lot of interest in which types choose which careers, you might consider showing them type tables, as described in "Using Type Tables in the Program" in section 5 (page 147).

Why are people put into boxes? *(This was asked when a facilitator decided to use type tables. See "Using Type Tables in the Program" in section 5, page 147, for suggested use of type tables.)*

People are often grouped together by their similarities such as by country of origin or ethnicity or by gender. However, when used incorrectly such groupings can be seen as stereotypical and limiting. If type is used to box people in then it is being *misused*. At its best, type can be used to anticipate communication problems.

The type table (grid with boxes) is like a bar graph or pie chart. It is used to show where numbers of different types are found (type distributions.) It can show types in the United States compared to types in another country or it can show which types seem to end up working in a certain careers.

My type guess is completely different from my MBTI results. What does that mean?

It may not mean anything at all. There are various reasons for differences between reported type and verified type. Differences like this can happen for as simple a reason as losing the sequence in filling out the bubbles on the answer sheet. Perhaps your votes were tallied inaccurately. (Some people try to trick the instrument by answering randomly or incorrectly.)

A difference between your preference and the preference described by the instrument may also be due to answering as you thought *someone* else would want you to answer. For example, you may decide you want to be different from how you are or that another person (a teacher or parent) wants you to be a certain way so you answer in that expected way. Or, as a young person, you may be exploring your identity and trying out different preferences.

Take this as an opportunity to use the type resources to continue exploring and remember that no instrument has the knowledge about yourself that you do. Only you can decide what type preferences fit you best.

What is the point of learning about type?

Learning about type can help us understand and change the way we communicate with others or make decisions. For example, instead of just learning how people with a preference for Introversion are different from people with a preference for Extraversion, we can ask ourselves questions such as these: "How do these ideas change the way I behave when I work with so and so?" or "What could I do differently to make everyone feel comfortable or to improve the way a group works?"

How does the MBTI instrument measure personality?

The Indicator doesn't really *measure* personality. It only *indicates* what your preferences *might be* based on the responses you gave on the Indicator. It points you in a possible direction. In a way, you vote for one preference or another each time you answer a question and the MBTI results are just a tally of your votes.

People are far too complex to be understood by any instrument. What the MBTI tool does is help people understand, accept, and appreciate their similarities and differences. In general you should be hesitant about accepting the results of any questionnaire over what you believe about yourself. This goes for the MBTI instrument, SATs, final exams, report cards, and any other assessments.

Do people always come out the same? Can people fake?

The MBTI questionnaire is a self-report instrument and a person may not answer the questions exactly the same every time. This can happen when people are still discovering themselves and experimenting. It can also happen if there is lack of trust about being forced to take it, about who will see the results, or how the results will be used. MBTI results may vary but that does not mean that a person's type changes.

There is no point in faking, since the results are for your use only. The prime goal is to discover a "best fit" for yourself regardless of what is reported by the MBTI results.

**Are any of the preferences better than the others? Why don't I like being told
I prefer Extraversion?**

Extraversion and Introversion are rarely used in the way Carl Jung intended. They are
often explained in ways that imply negative ideas. In type theory all of the preferences
and types are equal. Each brings gifts and challenges. If you feel uncomfortable when you
think of having a certain preference, ask yourself if it comes from some negative
interpretation of that preference, or some pressures in your environment. And remember, a
preference for Extraversion doesn't mean you *only* use that preference. You are able to use
all eight preferences, though you may prefer some over others.

How is the MBTI instrument a tool?

The ideas behind the MBTI instrument allow us to be aware of how we organize our
lives, take in information, and make decisions. It allows us to look at other ways of doing
those things and accept people who do things differently from us. We can be more deliberate
about what kinds of information we need to investigate. We can plan our time to allow for
curiosity, openness, and closure. We can feel good about ourselves without undervaluing
those who are different.

Unfortunately, some people choose to use type for stereotyping and making excuses.
Hopefully, our discussions will show you how unproductive this is. For example, when
someone says a certain type is cynical, smart, or unmotivated, that is based on one
person's experience. Type describes what you prefer, not what you are.

**Do ADD (Attention Deficit Disorder) and ADHD (Attention Deficit Hyperactivity
Disorder) relate to type?**

This is a tricky question for the following reasons: (1) Not everyone agrees that ADD is
a specific, diagnosable syndrome; (2) there are different kinds of ADD; (3) *all* young people
exhibit some of the behavior associated with attention deficits to some degree.

Studies have shown that no one type comes out as more likely to have ADD. A person who
prefers Extraversion is more likely *to be tagged as having* ADD/ADHD because they like to
move around, talk a lot, and often jump into things. But people who prefer Introversion
can also be labeled as having ADD because they tend to go inside their heads and not pay
attention to what is happening around them.

There are different kinds of Attention Deficit Hyperactivity Disorder (ADD/ ADHD). Since the mid-nineties it has been classified into subgroups: inattentive, predominantly hyperactive-impulsive, combined type and "not otherwise specified."

Data in a few published studies seem to show some type-related patterns but also raise questions. In a group of 152 children, the three most common types with ADD were found to be identical in the ADHD and control groups: ENFP 24%, ESFJ 18% and ESFP 15%. In another group of 110 children with attention difficulties, 57% preferred Introversion, 41% preferred Sensing, and 41% preferred Sensing as a dominant function. INFP, ISFJ, ISFP and ESFJ were more common than in the normative data, and, as in the normative data, ESFP was the most commonly preferred type and ESP was most frequent. This study found Introversion related to ADD and Extraversion to ADHD. Another author reported on early diagnoses of ADD and ADHD and asked if they were based on observations of young, immature expressions of EP preferences. Additional writers continue to question if educators, or the education culture, expect "quiet, organized" behaviors which is biased toward more IJ like preferences. Some people think that attention deficit labels may reveal differences between a child's type and the preferences of the adults who observe them while others question even the validity of ADD and ADHD (Alcock 2000).

How can the MBTI tool be used to improve world relations and personal relationships?

Isabel Myers developed the MBTI instrument with the hope that it would foster a culture based on "the constructive use of differences." If type can teach an individual that their way is not THE way, the amount of global conflict between governments and personal conflicts between people could be reduced.

Finally, you may hear comments such as the following:

- *I really don't believe what you said about the scores.*

- *I think if the scores show I had a high score on T then I would be good at that.*

- *It is good to have high scores.*

Comments such as these may come from teens in particular because they so often take tests built on trait theories, which measure the *amount* of a characteristic. So be prepared to explain the following points more than once: Indicator versus test, preference versus the way you are, and high scores do not mean skill or growth.

Reinforcing Learning About Type

At the end of a workshop, you may wish to capture what you have learned and reinforce the learning to keep type relevant for the participants in their daily lives.

Increasing the Payoff

The payoff of a type workshop is increased enormously when the messages about type are reinforced in the weeks and months that follow. By doing this you can show teens how the ideas behind type can make a difference in their lives. Following are some ideas to help you with follow-up activities.

- Design the program so you have an opportunity to work with the group again. Try to set up follow-up sessions, even just short ones on topics such as type and time management, or type and teams. These sessions should focus on practical applications rather than theory.

- If the group is ongoing, take advantage of any opportunity to reinforce type knowledge by weaving it into everyday activities of the group. If the group has a big decision to make, introduce the Zig-Zag model (see graphic below). If you would like more information on how to present the Zig-Zag model, please refer to the CAPT handout entitled "The Zig-Zag Process for Problem Solving" (Lawrence 2004). If the group is organizing a project, talk about the contributions of both Judging and Perceiving preferences.

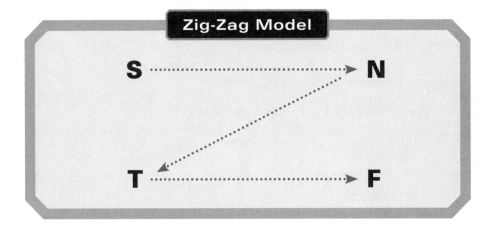

Zig-Zag Model

S ·····→ N

T ·····→ F

- If you don't work directly with the teens, coach the sponsor to use type in the group. Give a list of suggested type-in-action phrases to help the sponsor keep type alive easily. Create, with the sponsor, a list of common words and phrases used with the teens and talk about how they relate to the MBTI preferences.

- Consider sending notes (or e-mail messages), or a series of messages, to the participants, reinforcing some part of the type learning.

- If the participants are involved in college planning, talk to their counselors about how type concepts can help. Offer to do a type session for students soon to be involved in choosing a college.

- Look for ways to integrate type into homework coaching or offer to do a writing workshop based on type.

- Talk with school advisors about how type might be presented to their advisee groups.

- Whenever you propose using type with teens, try to gather information about a similar application somewhere else and use that information to show the value of type knowledge: Did it help a youth group decide on a fundraising project with fewer communication problems or conflicts? Did it help someone understand an adult better?

- Meet with teachers to talk about how type can be used in classroom management. When teachers use type techniques, encourage them to refer directly to what teens learned in the workshop.

- When you consistently use type concepts and ethics, teens begin to absorb them. Model type awareness by saying things such as the following:

  ▸ *I start with the general idea. Do you need more details?*

  ▸ *Let's give the Introverts a minute to think, and then we'll extravert about this question.*

  ▸ *I'm feeling uncomfortable with only looking at logic. I have a preference for Feeling, and I'd like to look at how this is going to affect people.*

  ▸ *I tend to work at the last minute. Is that going to make some of you nervous?*

- Talk to sports coaches or people running other extra-curricular activities about how type can be referred to and used.

- Try to give an introductory type presentation to parents, which doesn't include the Indicator itself but presents the concept of preferences and some examples of type in action.

- Give a type presentation for teachers and administrative staff.

- If there is a peer mediation or conflict program in your school or community, meet with the sponsors and show them how type might help.

- Provide students with a reading list of type-related books and materials, and direct them to Web sites about type, particularly **www.typecan.com**, a site that was developed by teens for teens.

Capturing Your Learning

- Gather all the relevant data about your presentation while it is fresh. Record the year, the number of youths in the individual groups and the aggregate group, the number and genders of students in each group, plus any other characteristics that you see as relevant such as students that are twins, hearing impaired students, or students for whom English is a second language. Keep all the feedback forms. This material will be useful in several ways:

  ▸ You may decide to study this information at a later time for your own use in writing about type or to use for research.

  ▸ You may wish to send validated type results along with demographic information to the Center for Applications of Psychological Type (CAPT) for entry into the comprehensive data base where it will be available to researchers and other members of the type community. CAPT is particularly interested in data on teens and type. See page 183 for information on data submission.

  ▸ Keep comments that were written on newsprint or other visuals to use as material in future workshops or to share among teens in other settings.

- Keep a journal of your experiences. Note what went well and what you would change and why. Your experiences could become an opportunity for long-term work, and your notes can provide guidance for yourself or someone else.

2
organizing the program

2

organizing the program

Setting Up the Workshop

Following are some general guidelines and suggestions for organizing, scheduling, and planning an MBTI workshop for teens. More detailed step-by-step instructions are presented in sections 3 and 4.

Contract with the Sponsors

An MBTI workshop for teenagers begins long before the actual session. The first step is to lay a foundation of understanding and commitment with the adults in charge and the parents of those who will participate. The workshop may be presented in a school class, a youth group, a church group, a social service or recreational group, or some other organization. Before committing to present the workshop, you will need to establish whether this is the right application of type for this group. Cover the following points with the adults sponsoring the session.

- Why do they want to use the MBTI tool? Does someone want to "type" the students and if so why? Do they plan to reinforce and use the ideas of psychological type after the workshop?

- Is there a problem to be solved? What is it and how would MBTI results be used? Remind the sponsors that MBTI results are not used to sort students for placement or selection.

- Is the MBTI session being considered as part of a larger curriculum? If so, how will it fit in?

- Has the MBTI instrument been used before and how did the experience go? Do the participants have any preconceived notions about the MBTI use?

- Do students or their parents need to sign a permission slip or release form before they complete the MBTI questionnaire? Be sure the sponsors are up to date on state, school, and local regulations regarding the use of instruments like the MBTI tool with adolescents. The release should state the nature and purpose of your visit and what will become of the information. (If you plan to use a video camera you may need additional permission.)

  ▶ A sample letter (RM-1) for explaining to students, parents, and other concerned individuals what the Indicator is and how it will be used is provided on the CD-ROM with other resource materials. The letter can also be read aloud to students when you administer the MBTI questionnaire.

- Do the sponsors realize that MBTI results go only to the student and will be shared with others only if the student chooses to do so? This may come as a surprise in educational settings where results are most often used by adults to make decisions about children.

- Do they understand that taking the MBTI instrument must be voluntary with no pressure exerted? Teenagers can still take the workshop (and get a great deal out of it) if they decline to take the instrument. (Such refusals are, however, rare.)

- Are teachers, adult advisors or leaders willing to take the MBTI instrument and receive the results with the teens? Set the expectations that any adults who want the results must attend the whole workshop. You wouldn't want their participation to inhibit the young people so first determine if joint teen-adult participation is common to the group's culture. Invite them to take an "actor" role. Adult participation heightens variety, interest, and animation, especially when they perform in the skits.

- Review with the sponsors the ethical guidelines for administering the instrument and giving feedback (see chapter 7, page 185). Additional ethical guidelines are available in books such as *Building People, Building Programs* (Lawrence and Martin 2001) and *People Types & Tiger Stripes* (Lawrence 2009) or through the Myers & Briggs Foundation (**www.myersbriggs.org**) or the Center for Applications of Psychological Type (**www.capt.org**).

- Be prepared to explain why you use the MBTI tool over other instruments. Refer sponsors to *Buros Mental Measurement Yearbook* for an objective comparison of the MBTI and other Jungian-based personality instruments. Or you may refer them to the Instrument Comparison Checklist from the Association for Psychological Type International (see Resources, page 188).

- Are sponsors aware of the cost of using the instrument?

- Have the sponsors allowed enough time for you to administer the MBTI instrument (in a separate session) and hold a full feedback workshop of four hours. If they do not feel such time can be made available, consider presenting the workshop without administering the MBTI instrument, allowing students to self-assess their preferences.

- Do the sponsors realize that the absolute maximum group size for the workshop is 25? If they have more, then two sessions should be scheduled either simultaneously with two facilitators, or at different times. Ideally, a group should be large enough to provide type diversity but not so large that it discourages participation. Explain that in large groups, the opportunity to address misconceptions and specific questions is often lost.

I learned that my preferences included Introversion. That explains why I seem to need a certain amount of time to myself. To recharge.

Provide for Special Requirements

- Find out if any of the participants have special requirements, e.g., sight impairment, reading level below eighth grade, learning difficulties, or English as a second language. (See "Administering the MBTI® Instrument" on page 37 for how to deal with these situations.)

- Consider whether you, as the facilitator, will need the help of someone more experienced in working with teenagers or more knowledgeable about the issues and needs of this age group.

- If the presentation is part of a course where the students will be held accountable for the material, find out what information needs to be included in written handouts for future review.

- Find out if special permissions are needed or if there are any additional people who you need to brief about the workshop and the administration of the MBTI instrument.

Know Your Audience

Before the workshop begins, you should try to gather the following information. Some of this information may come naturally from talking to participants during the administration of the MBTI instrument.

- Have these teenagers had experience with similar instruments or similar workshops? How do they feel about that experience? Has it left them with concerns or questions you need to clear up before the workshop?

- What issues may be sensitive to the members of this group. Sometimes group members know about romantic relationships, conflicts, or sensitive issues in the group.

> **There may be special circumstances in the group that influence your activities. For example, we sometimes use a decision-making exercise which is based on a person who had a child with leukemia. In one session there was a teen in a group who had a sibling with that illness. We were able to choose a different exercise.**

- Some young people are turned off by the terms "teenager" and "teen." They may prefer "youth," "young people," or "high schoolers." Find out what language is best for your situation.

- If you plan to alter or add to activities or materials in this module, consider using a few teens you know as a focus group to give general advice about activities, cartoons, movie clips, etc. Sometimes they don't react to ideas the way you anticipate, and you can avoid an awkward moment in the session by testing your ideas first.

Check out the Facility

Make arrangements to visit the room beforehand and arrange for any changes. The room should have the following:

- A space as open and flexible as possible, allowing room for participants to move around into small groups, facilitate "fishbowl exercises," and work at flip charts.
- Two or three chairs on each side of the easel for fishbowl activities (never use more than six volunteers)
- Lighting that will not cast a glare on the screen during visual presentations.
- Tables (if available), preferably round, for the participants to work at.
- A table or desk at the front of the room for the facilitator to arrange materials.
- If the following items are not provided by the facility, you should arrange to provide them for the presentation.
    - LCD (or overhead) projector and screen or white wall.
    - TV, VCR, or DVD player if you plan to use videos or movies.
    - At least two easels with flip charts.
- Check fire regulations if you plan to use the candle exercise (see unit 3, "Sensing and Intuition," page 89).

Gather Materials and Supplies

General Supplies

- LCD (or overhead projector)
- Extra bulb for projector
- DVD player or VCR if using the alternate exercise
- Colored markers
- Masking tape
- Agenda or outline on newsprint to be posted throughout the workshop
- Small travel alarm clock/watch for timing exercises/activities
- Type table (RM-2)
- Four to six chairs, divided on either side of the easel for fishbowl activities
- A selection of type books for people to consult during and after the workshop (You also may want to loan or donate a few good books to the group sponsors, for people who want to do more reading about type.)
- A bowl of wrapped candies: two very different kinds
- Pencil for each student

Props for the workshop

- V-1, the *What Do You See? visual* projected on the screen

- A large type table, posted (can be purchased through CAPT, www.capt.org)

- Agenda, posted

- Favorite quotes about type, such as the quote found at the beginning of *Gifts Differing* by Isabel Briggs Myers, posted

- Handouts at each place (see handout list in following section)

- Pencil at each place

- Bowl of candy with only two kinds of candy and a sign that says, "Please take just ONE piece"

- A candle, candle holder, and matches for the S–N exercise or some other prop if the fire regulations prohibit the lighting of a candle

- Posters showing different animals and people getting along, posted

- Choose a poster for the S–N exercise

- Music

- Sixteen packages wrapped in different styles (to be used later to reinforce the idea that each type offers special gifts)

- Very large sunglasses like the ones worn by clowns with the letters "M-B-T-I" printed on the lenses (to reinforce the concept that the MBTI instrument gives you another way of looking at the world)

- A version of the history of psychological type

- Books on personality type for teens

- Koosh balls or small stuffed animal for the speaker to hold during discussions

Handouts for Each Student

- One set of worksheets per participant, *First Guess Type* (PM-1) and *Who Influences You?* (PM-2). (Refer to the CD-ROM that accompanies this book.)

- An envelope for each participant that contains the *Participant Feedback Packet* (PM-4), with the following information: the participant's MBTI instrument results, recorded on the worksheet "Finding the Type That Fits You;" a set of the sixteen type descriptions; and a separate page titled "Now That You Know About Type."

Personal Teaching Notes

- LCD slides or overheads made from materials provided in this program.

- Flip charts you have created with agendas, exercise instructions, or groups assignments.

- PowerPoint® type presentation if you plan to use one.

- Type table on regular paper with check marks in boxes rather than names of participants.

- Notes on who marked their answer sheet "0," and therefore prefers to be an "observer" (see page 39).

Administering the MBTI® Instrument

Preparation

1. Assemble enough Indicators and answer sheets for all the participants plus any sponsors or other adults who also plan to take it.

2. Prepare a letter describing the workshop and the administration and use of the Indicator (see RM-1). The letter can be used in several ways:

   - Sent to parents so they know what is going on (an actual permission form is included in RM-1).

   - Sent as an explanation to administrators or other involved adults.

   - Reviewed with students at the administration session.

3. Find out if you will have to adapt the administration process for any of the following reasons:

   - *A sight-impaired teen.* Consult the *MBTI® Manual* for how to read the questionnaire in a nonbiased way.

   - *A teen who does not speak English as a first language.* The MBTI questionnaire is available in many languages or you can allow extra time if it seems appropriate.

   - *A teen with reading or learning disabilities.* You can allow extra time or consult the teacher about how to adapt the process.

   - *A teen who is test adverse.* Adaptations can be made for someone who has received so much negative information from paper evaluations that he or she may refuse to take the instrument.

- *A teen who does not read at the eighth-grade level.* You can use the Murphy-Meisgeier Type Indicator for Children® (MMTIC®) instrument as an option in this case. This instrument was designed for use with children in grades two through seven. (For more information, contact the publisher, Center for Applications of Psychological Type (CAPT) at www.capt.org.)

- *A teen that cannot be present at the MBTI administration session.* You should push hard for all students to attend. If there is no alternative, you may meet individually with students who cannot be at the session. If you are available to meet separately with a student, then let the teen be responsible for setting up a time to take the MBTI instrument and receive feedback. If the Indicator must be administered without you, then be sure that the person administering the instrument is MBTI certified. Finally, if all other avenues have been exhausted for the teen to be able to take the instrument, you can have the student come to the workshop and participate with the understanding that he or she will not receive a feedback packet.

Make any of these special arrangements in advance so a student will not be embarrassed during the session. These students, like all participants, should also be told they have the option of not taking the Indicator, but assured that they will still learn a great deal from attending the workshop.

Administering the MBTI® Instrument and Setting the Tone

Before the workshop, you will need to meet with the participants for 60 to 75 minutes to administer the Instrument. This is also a good opportunity to set a friendly open tone for the workshop. Try to have a room with individual desks so that students will not converse while taking the Instrument.

Schedule this meeting before the workshop allowing enough time for scoring the Indicators (about 15 to 20 minutes per Indicator). If you are sending the Indicators out for scoring, be sure that you plan ahead so the results can be returned to you in time for the workshop. This initial session is also an opportunity for mutual introductions and for teens to ask questions about the Indicator and the workshop.

Do not allow this administration meeting to be facilitated by anyone else (except if absolutely necessary, by another MBTI certified practitioner). We have learned from experience that inevitably people who are not invested in the workshop or knowledgeable about the MBTI instrument are not able to set the proper tone, make the important points regarding the process, or get all the forms back. They may inadvertently create doubts about confidentiality and unconsciously violate principles such as explaining words on the instrument.

Administer and score the Indicators, using templates, computer software, or an outside scoring service. Remember to note elsewhere the names of students who put "O" (for observer) on their answer sheets so you can honor their request. Then erase the "O" if you send the answer sheets to be machine scored. If a student did not complete the Indicator at all, make a note that he or she will not receive feedback.

Enter each participant's MBTI results on the worksheet titled "Finding the Type That Fits You," which is page 2 of the *Participant Feedback Packet* (PM-4), that you will distribute to each student.

Review Results

Note any unusual results and double-check scoring if necessary. If a participant did not fill in enough answers to get valid feedback, make a note to explain what that means in terms of type reporting.

Create a Type Table

When you have the results, make a type table for your own use. Think about the implications of the type mix in this group. Will participation be strong? Will the group want structure? Will one type or preference tend to dominate? Will one type or preference feel isolated? This analysis can be invaluable in fine-tuning your teaching plan and anticipating obstacles. This type table is for your use only. If you decide to use type tables in the program, see "Using Type Tables in Options and Adaptations" in section 5, page 147.

Separate the answer sheets marked with an "O" for Observer so you know not to put them in a fishbowl group. Several exercises in the program are fishbowl activities in which some participants perform actions (discuss, plan, etc.) while the rest of the class observes.

Create groups for exercises based on results. If you are making up groups of people who share a preference, choose those people who had the clearest preference score on that dichotomy.

> **fyi**
>
> Once we were approached by two guidance counselors working with a group of teens identified as "at risk for dropping out of school." Since the opportunity required travel, it seemed to make sense to save time and cost by having the counselors administer the MBTI instrument. The group refused to fill out the Indicator. We found out too late that these teens had only learned about their deficiencies whenever they filled out bubbles on paper. So when given the opportunity to take the MBTI instrument, they wanted no part of another "test." The enthusiastic but untrained counselors were unprepared to illustrate how the Indicator was unlike other questionnaires. As a result of that experience, we administer the MBTI instrument ourselves, and when necessary we build in exercises and discussion to eliminate or reduce concerns and fears. Most often there is no additional fee for this part of the work.

Introduce the Program

Step 1 Briefly introduce yourself and tell why you are there. Tell a little about the format of the workshop and the types of activities that participants can expect. Be sure to make the following points about the workshop.

- You will be looking at differences in the way people approach life, take in information, and make decisions. There is no right way, and participants will not be evaluated in any way.

- Most teens find the information very useful in understanding themselves and other people.

- The workshop will be interactive with lots of moving around and working in groups.

Explain that part of the workshop includes an opportunity to take the Myers-Briggs Type Indicator assessment, which will provide feedback about personality type. The Indicator results are not the final word on their personality type; they simply give participants interesting input. Stress the following:

- You are not required to take the Indicator. Most people do, but you can still get a lot out of the session if you choose not to take the instrument.

- You must attend the whole workshop to receive your results. Results cannot be mailed or otherwise sent to you without a face-to-face interpretation. You must attend the workshop or make an appointment with me to spend at least an hour and a half going over the results face-to-face or by phone.

- If there is more than one absentee, then we will meet as a group for a makeup session.
- The results of the MBTI instrument are only shared with you, and only you have the option to share the results with others if you wish to. This means the results do not go in your file, or to your teachers or your parents. You can also say something such as, "If I ever want to talk to someone else about your type, I will need to get your written permission first."

Step 2 Pass out the Indicators and the answer sheets and tell the participants the following:

- Do not write in the booklet, only on the answer sheet.

- Be sure to put your name and gender on the answer sheet (and any other information you want them to provide).

- If you do not wish to take the MBTI instrument, you can simply mark "O" (for observer) in the upper right hand corner of the answer sheet and turn it in.

- If you take the MBTI instrument but do not wish to volunteer for any fishbowl exercises, you should complete the Indicator but also mark "O," indicating you only want to observe in those exercises.

Step 3 Review the cover letter and the instructions on the front of the Indicator booklet. Say the following:

- The Indicator should be taken in a relaxed mode.

- The Indicator is not a "test" for the following reasons:
  ‣ There are no right or wrong answers. In other words, there are no better or worse types to be.
  ‣ You can reject the results if you like.
  ‣ The results are only given to the respondent.

- Don't spend too much time on any one answer. No one answer will change the results dramatically.

- Remember to answer as you actually prefer, not as you think you should.

- Be honest. The results will be much more interesting that way, and no one but you will see the results unless you choose to share them.

- Try not to skip any questions as the results will not be as helpful to you.

Some of my friends wait until the last minute to start their projects. When I try I get really stressed and can't think.

Step 4 While students are completing the Indicator, remain available for clarification of directions but do not interpret or translate the meaning of any questions. The MBTI instrument is not timed, but it generally takes between 30 and 60 minutes to complete. Do not pressure people to hurry and ask those who have finished to sit quietly or leave the room so they won't disturb others. If students are not allowed to leave the room, consider having some pre-reading or another task available to keep them busy while the others complete their instruments.

Some teens may not pay attention as you give directions, so you will need to repeat instructions as they work through the items. It is helpful to show a visual of the answer sheet (on a LCD or overhead), highlighting the parts you want filled in and showing where to put the "O" for observer.

The booklets should be returned with the answer sheets. Let participants know if there is a replacement fee for lost booklets.

You may want to invite the teens to contact you by phone or e-mail if they have any questions.

The MBTI® Self-scorable Instrument

The self-scorable version of the MBTI instrument is an option. The authors prefer not to use it for the following reasons:

- Although the self-scorable Indicator is a valid version of the instrument, we feel its use gives students the impression of a "quick and dirty" quiz rather than a thoughtful serious instrument.

- It takes time away from the actual session. Since time is often limited, we prefer to use the time for a more complete explanation of type and how to use the MBTI results. However, if you have students complete the self-scorable Indicator before coming to the session, this particular drawback is not a problem.

- Use of the self-scorable version does not allow the facilitator to have information in advance about the makeup of the group in order to make appropriate adjustments to the plan of presentation.

- Taking the instrument within the session may interrupt the flow of presentation and discussion, which can begin a session on an awkward note, in our opinion.

- In addition, since time is limited, taking the self-scorable in the session puts pressure on those who need more time or special arrangements. Therefore, the use of self-scorable heightens the problems of someone who may already feel self-conscious. Such pressure may impact those people's results.

PART TWO

program

3

facilitator preparation

3

facilitator's preparation

Overview of the Workshop

This is an introductory program that presents psychological type and Myers-Briggs Type Indicator® (MBTI®) results to teens as a way to gain self-knowledge. The design of the program takes into account the teen stage of development, the issues in teens' lives, and their need to manage human interactions.

It is appropriate for use in academic classes, youth groups, extra-curricular groups, counseling groups, or any other similar setting. The group does not have to be intact or ongoing.

The program is designed to follow the administration of the MBTI tool to the teen participants. We have found that the attention level of the participants and their understanding of the MBTI tool are far greater when personal feedback is provided.

The program requires 4 hours (includes two 15-minute breaks), plus a pre-session to administer the MBTI instrument. It can be delivered in one half-day session or several shorter ones (see page 145).

The Teaching Model

The program is divided into seven units: an introductory unit, four units to introduce the four pairs of psychological type preferences, a feedback unit in which students establish their best fit type, and an applications unit that helps teens use type in their daily lives.

The principles of type differences are used in the design of the units. As the introduction of each preference pair is a process of taking in information, we use a method that honors both the Sensing function and the Intuiting function while using the type table quadrants as a learning cycle.

As each pair is introduced, the IS quadrant is engaged first with a concrete experience. This is usually an exercise allowing the teens to observe type in action: a fishbowl exercise, skit, or whole group experience.

Next, we move to the IN quadrant by summarizing the theory and explaining the meaning behind the differences which they have just observed. We use a series of illustrations to summarize the theory. (Remember, if you decide to add additional cartoons or illustrations, you may need to get permission from the artists.)

Then we explore the EN quadrant and what can be done with this new knowledge. Finally, and most important, we move to the ES quadrant with an application to real life.

In addition, we model positive references to all types, avoiding stereotyping or "type-bashing" of any kind.

In introducing each of the four preference pairs, the program provides four elements:

1. An exercise demonstrating the preference pair in action.

2. A presentation, using overheads or PowerPoint® visuals with illustrations of each preference and differences between them.

3. A *First Guess Type* worksheet (PM-1) by each participant of his or her preference in this pair.

4. An exercise applying this preference pair to real life.

For S–N and J–P, the application exercise occurs immediately after the *First Guess Type* worksheet activity. For E–I and T–F, the application exercise comes in the final unit, after the participants have received feedback and have determined their best-fit type.

In presenting the preference pairs, it is critical to make clear how each preference shows up in the everyday life of young people:

- The E–I pair helps clarify different social life needs and response times in school.

- The S–N pair is helpful in examining personal and academic discussions: teacher's questions, student responses, and differing test expectations between teachers.

- The T–F pair sheds light on differences at home, with social and school issues, and in grappling with ethical questions.

- The J–P pair helps clarify differences in completing tasks and in social or academic planning.

Programs for teens require a high degree of participation and activity to maintain interest. We have therefore designed the program to move quickly, involve participants, and allow teens to move around, engaging in a variety of activities. You may find that some of the basics of adult programs, such as introductions and presentation of agenda and goals, are abbreviated here. In our experience, teens were uniformly turned off by these activities, preferring to jump straight to the point.

Program Objectives

At the end of the program, participants should be able to do the following:

- Understand the concepts, terms, and background of psychological type and the MBTI instrument.

- Connect to the positive focus of personality differences and the importance of valuing differences and using type knowledge constructively.

- View psychological type as a positive means to understand themselves and others.

- Have some idea of how type impacts their relationships with family, teachers, and peers.

- Have established at least a preliminary idea of what their individual preferences are and how they can be used for self-management.

- Observe type preferences reflected in the thoughts and actions of people around them.

- Have specific ideas of how they might use type knowledge to interact positively with others in their lives.

The following points should be emphasized whenever there is an opportunity in the program. They should be mentioned more than once and interwoven into the discussions and summaries wherever possible.

- The preferences are inborn.

- We can use either preference, but usually choose our favored one.

- All types are valuable.

- Type is about normal healthy differences—not "problems."

- Type is not meant to limit anyone or tell people what to do.

- Type is only part of the story—it does not explain everything.

- You can't really know another's type preferences, and it can be perceived as invasive if you guess someone's preferences or tell people what you think their preferences are.

My friends notice that I really pay attention to details. I seem to do it without even thinking about it.

Flow and Timing

Timing for the program is based on 20 to 25 participants per session. We *strongly* recommend, based on testing the program, that you not go beyond that number. If you have more participants, schedule a second session or two simultaneous sessions with two facilitators.

Unit 1: Introduction . . . . 20 minutes

Unit 2: Extraversion and Introversion . . . . 30 minutes

BREAK .15 minutes

Unit 3: Sensing and Intuition . . . . 30 minutes

Unit 4: Thinking and Feeling . . . . 30 minutes

BREAK .15 minutes

Unit 5: Judging and Perceiving. . . . . 35 minutes

Unit 6: What's Your Type . . . . 15 minutes

Unit 7: Type In Real Life . . . . 50 minutes

Total Time (*including two breaks*) . . . . **4 hours**

Unit-By-Unit Timing*

Unit 1: Introduction

Total Time: 20 minutes

> **Step 1**: Participants arrive. (10 minutes)
>
> **Step 2**: Discuss *What Do You See?* visual. (2 minutes)
>
> **Step 3**: Debrief candy choices. (1 minute)
>
> **Step 4**: *Who Are You?* (1 minute)
>
> **Step 5**: Handwriting exercise. (4 minutes)
>
> **Step 6**: Introduce type preferences and agenda. (2 minutes)

Unit 2: Introducing Extraversion and Introversion

Total Time: 30 minutes

> **Step 1**: Conduct the fishbowl exercise: *Grading for Participation*. (15 minutes)
>
> **Step 2**: Debrief fishbowl exercise. (5 minutes)
>
> **Step 3**: Introduce the E–I preferences. (5 minutes)
>
> **Step 4**: Ask participants to complete worksheets. (5 minutes)

Unit 3: Introducing Sensing and Intuition

Total Time: 30 minutes

> **Step 1**: Conduct the candle exercise. (5 minutes)
>
> **Step 2**: Introduce the S–N preferences. (5 minutes)
>
> **Step 3**: Ask participants to complete worksheets. (5 minutes)
>
> **Step 4**: Conduct the poster exercise. (10 minutes)
>
> **Step 5**: Summarize the poster exercise. (5 minutes)

Locations of specific materials are presented in section 4.

Unit 4: Introducing Thinking and Feeling

Total Time: 30 minutes

Step 1: Conduct the fishbowl exercise: *Who Stays Home?* (10 minutes)

Step 2: Discuss the fishbowl exercise. (10 minutes)

Step 3: Introduce the T–F preferences. (5 minutes)

Step 4: Ask participants to complete worksheets. (5 minutes)

Unit 5: Introducing Judging and Perceiving

Total Time: 35 minutes

Step 1: Present skit: *The Paper Is Due!* (10 minutes)

Step 2: Debrief the skit. (5 minutes)

Step 3: Introduce the J–P preferences. (5 minutes)

Step 4: Ask participants to complete worksheets. (5 minutes)

Step 5: Conduct application exercise: *The Line-Up*. (10 minutes)

Unit 6: What's Your Type?

Total Time: 15 minutes

Step 1: Introduce type dynamics and the concept of captain and first mate. (2 minutes)

Step 2: Introduce the best-fit process. (2 minutes)

Step 3: Individual exercise: best-fit type. (10 minutes)

Step 4: Summarize the best-fit process. (1 minute)

Unit 7: Type in Real Life

Total Time: 50 minutes

> **Step 1**: E–I application exercise: *Managing Your Energy.* (20 minutes)
>
> **Step 2**: Conduct application exercise: *Can I Use the Car?* (20 minutes)
>
> **Step 3**: What Has Been Learned. (5 minutes)
>
> **Step 4**: Review: "Now That You Know About Type." (2 minutes)
>
> **Step 5**: Read the monologue: "What Might Happen Next Tuesday." (2 minutes)
>
> **Step 6**: Thanks and evaluations. (1 minute)

Preparation for Each Unit

(NOTE: Review these preparatory steps before presenting each unit. Unit presentations begin on page 65.)

Unit 1: Introduction

(Unit 1 begins on page 69. Time: 20 minutes.)

Why Do This Unit?

1. To pique the interest of the participants about psychological type.

2. To position type as a way of valuing differences and respecting the gifts of each individual.

3. To give participants an idea of the origins of the Myers-Briggs Type Indicator instrument.

Experience has shown without any doubt that this first unit MUST MOVE QUICKLY. Experienced facilitators will be tempted to begin with detailed introductions, background material about type, and lots of information about type and what it can do. RESIST THIS TEMPTATION. We urge you to follow the timing and flow shown here. Otherwise, teens will turn off because the session will start to sound too much like school or other situations in which people talk at them.

Preparation for Unit 1

A. Decide what physical arrangements will best invite the participants as they enter the room. Gather the props you want to use. These should appeal to auditory, visual, and kinesthetic learning styles and might include the following:

- *What Do You See?* (V-1) projected on the screen

- A large type table, posted

- Agenda, posted

- Favorite quotes about type, such as the quote found at the beginning of *Gifts Differing* by Isabel Briggs Myers, posted

- Handouts (*First Guess Type* [PM-1] and *Who Influences You?* [PM-2]) at each place

- Pencil at each place

- Bowl of candy with only two kinds of candy and a sign that says, "Please take just ONE piece"

- A candle, candle holder, and match for the S–N exercise or some other prop if the fire regulations prohibit the lighting of a candle

- Posters that show different animals and people getting along, posted

- A poster for the S–N exercise that is interesting and contains an overall theme plus details

- Music

- Sixteen packages wrapped in different styles (to reinforce the idea that each type offers special gifts)

- Very large sunglasses like the ones worn by clowns, with the letters "M-B-T-I" printed on the lenses to reinforce the idea that the MBTI instrument gives you another way of looking at the world

- A version of the history of psychological type

- Books on personality type for teens

- Koosh balls or small stuffed animal for the speaker to hold during discussions

B. If people in the group don't know each other, plan a short icebreaker to encourage interaction. This should be something physical and fast moving (see example in section 5).

C. Test your plan to use props and humor with someone the same age as the participants, in order to identify ideas that may be corny, childish, too sophisticated, or preachy.

D. Project the *What Do You See?* visual (V-1) so that students can see it as soon as they enter the room.

E. Review your plan for the session to be sure you include activities that appeal to all preferences. You can point this out to participants as they become familiar with the preferences.

F. Choose examples of teens being pressured to act against their preferences (for use with handwriting exercises in step 5).

G. Decide how you will introduce yourself. Try to work into your self-introduction points about ways you have found the MBTI tool helpful, how teenagers you know have used the MBTI tool, and how you have worked with teens and type in the past.

H. Review visuals V-1 through V-3 for use in this unit.

Unit 2: Introducing Extraversion and Introversion

(Unit 2 begins on page 79. Time: 30 minutes.)

Why Do This Unit?

1. For teens to see what Extraversion and Introversion look like in real life.

2. To explain what Extraversion and Introversion mean in terms of psychological type theory.

3. To let teens make an educated guess about which of this pair they prefer.

4. For teens to see how knowing about Extraversion and Introversion may help them in their lives.

Preparation for Unit 2

A. Prepare a flip chart that reads:

> *The teachers of your school are proposing to have 25% of your grade based on class participation. What is your response to this idea?*

Have another blank flip chart ready for the discussion.

B. For the fishbowl exercise, select one group of four Extraverts and one group of four Introverts based on Indicator scores of people in the workshop. If you don't have four of one preference, then just make the groups of equal size. (Do not use anyone who put an "0" on the Indicator answer sheet.)

C. Review the E–I unit visuals V-4, V-5, and V-6A through V-6G, including the wording that can help you introduce the E–I cartoons ("Suggested Scripts for Explaining Visuals," page 176).

D. Choose additional cartoons that you may want to use in your presentation. Be very careful that none of the cartoons demeans one preference over another, even subtly.

E. Think about which examples or anecdotes about E and I preferences from your own experience or from other classes may be helpful to use in your explanation. Test these examples to be sure they do not favor one preference over the other. Use teen examples wherever possible.

F. Have *First Guess Type* (PM-1) and the *Who Influences You?* (PM-2) worksheets for each participant (if you did not put them out on desks in advance).

G. To explain the *Who Influences You?* worksheet, prepare examples of how people in a teen's environment might convey the message that one of the E–I preferences is better or best.

H. Make a flip chart with the discussion questions for the fishbowl exercise.

Unit 3: Introducing Sensing and Intuition

(Unit 3 begins on page 89. Time: 30 minutes.)

Why Do This Unit?

1. To allow participants to see what the Sensing and Intuitive preferences look like in real life.

2. To explain the meaning of Sensing and Intuition in psychological type theory.

3. To have participants make educated guesses as to their preferences in this pair.

Preparation for Unit 3

A. Get out candle, holder, match (or other prop if fire regulations prevent the use of a candle), and empty flip chart for recording comments.

B. Set out flip-chart paper and markers for each small group for the poster exercise.

C. Review the S–N visuals V-4, V-5, and V-7A through V-7G, including the wording that will help you introduce V-7A through V-7G ("Suggested Scripts for Explaining Visuals," page 177).

D. Choose cartoons you may want to use, taking care that none of the cartoons puts down one preference, even subtly.

E. Choose examples or anecdotes about S and N preferences from your own experience or from other classes may be helpful in your explanation. Test these examples to be sure they do not favor one preference over the other. Use teen examples wherever possible.

F. For explaining the *Who Influences You?* worksheet, prepare examples of how the people in a teen's environment may convey the message that one of the S or N preferences is better or best.

G. Obtain a poster for appropriate use in an S–N exercise. The poster should have some detailed elements that can be discerned by Sensing types but also contain a sweeping message that would be noted by an Intuitive type. Artists whose works may be of interest for this exercise include Salvador Dali, M.C. Escher, Paul Klee, or appropriate works of Henri Rousseau.

Unit 4: Introducing Thinking and Feeling

(Unit 4 begins on page 99. Time: 30 minutes.)

Why Do This Unit?

1. To allow participants to see what the Thinking and Feeling preferences look like in real life.

2. To explain the meaning of Thinking and Feeling in psychological type.

3. To have participants make educated guesses about their preferences in this pair.

Preparation for Unit 4

A. Review the written scenario for the exercise, *Who Stays Home?*

B. Select students for the fishbowl groups—four students for the Thinking group and four students from the Feeling group—based on their Indicator results. Record their names in your workshop notes. Remember not to select students who wrote "0" on their answer sheets.

C. Review the T–F unit visuals V-4, V-5, and V-8A through V-8G, including the wording that will help you introduce V-8A through V-8G ("Suggested Scripts for Explaining Visuals," page 179).

D. Choose cartoons you may want to use. Be careful that none of the cartoons demeans one preference, even subtly.

E. Think about which examples or anecdotes about T and F preferences from your own experience or from other classes may be helpful in your explanation. Test these examples to be sure they do not favor one preference over the other. Use teen examples wherever possible.

F. You might want to review *In a Different Voice,* other works by Carol Gilligan, as well as research on development and gender because the types of issues in these works may come up during the unit.

G. Think of specific examples of how teens may be influenced by other people to believe they should prefer either Thinking or Feeling.

Unit 5: Introducing Judging and Perceiving

(Unit 5 begins on page 109. Time: 35 minutes.)

Why Do This Unit?

1. To allow participants to see what the Judging and Perceiving preference look like in real life.

2. To explain the meaning of Judging and Perceiving in psychological type theory.

3. To have participants make educated guesses about their preferences in this pair.

Preparation for Unit 5

A. Review the leader's guide and the script for the skit *The Paper is Due!* (RM-3). Choose actors for the skit. Using teachers or other adults is fun, plus it models adults being open and accepting about personality type. If you decide to use students, do not use anyone who put an "O" on their Indicator answer sheet. Check with your actors to see if they are willing.

B. Brief the actors ahead of time and give them each a set of the nine-page dialogue.

C. Gather the props for the skit: assignment book, calendar, index cards, and two toy telephones.

D. Consider reviewing the book *Procrastination* by Judith Provost, since the subject of procrastination often comes up in the skit.

E. Review the J–P unit visuals V-4, V-5, and V-9A through V-9G, including the wording that will help you introduce V-9A through V-9G ("Suggested Scripts for Explaining Visuals," pages 179–180).

F. Choose any cartoons you may want to use. Be careful that none of the cartoons puts down one preference, even subtly.

G. Think about which examples or anecdotes about J–P from your own experience or from other classes may be helpful in your explanation. Test these examples to be sure they do not favor one preference over the other. Use teen examples wherever possible.

H. Create some examples of how teens may be influenced by peers, family members, or authority figures to prefer Judging or Perceiving.

I. Locate a long space where all the participants can line up at one time. Mark the line with masking tape or some other material. Then mark one end with the number 1 and the other end with the number 30.

Unit 6: What's Your Type?

(Unit 6 begins on page 121. Time: 15 minutes.)

Why Do This Unit?

1. To give participants the results of their Indicators and explain these results.

2. To have participants explore why the types on their *First Guess Type* worksheets and their Indicator results may differ.

3. To convey to participants that they are the final judges of their type and they are under no pressure to make a final decision about their types until they feel ready.

4. To have participants explore how their environments might influence them to report—and to try to use—preferences that are not their natural ones.

Preparation for Unit 6

A. Check that the MBTI results have been entered on the "Finding the Type That Fits You Best" worksheet in PM-4 for each participant, and that the name of each teen is on the outside of each packet.

B. Review Unit 6 visuals V-10 through V-14.

Unit 7: Type in Real Life

(Unit 7 begins on page 131. Time: 50 minutes.)

Why Do This Unit?

1. To allow participants to practice applying the type preferences to situations in their own lives.

2. To deepen the participants' understanding of the type preferences.

3. To help participants anticipate how they might find themselves using type in their lives.

4. To point out some of the pitfalls of using type and how to avoid them.

5. To summarize the most important lessons about type from the workshop.

Preparation for Unit 7

A. Review the written scenario for the application exercise, *Can I Use the Car?* (page 134). Decide whether you need to tailor it for younger teens.

B. Make handouts for the E–I exercise: *Managing Your Energy* (PM-3).

C. Review the contents of "Now That You Know About Type" in PM-4.

D. Review the monologue script "What Might Happen Next Tuesday" (page 138). Decide on any modifications of the script to reflect this group and its environment.

4

unit-by-unit presentation

4

unit-by-unit presentation

The following icon key is for use with the step-by-step units of the MBTI presentation for teens. The program is designed in an easy-to-follow format, and these icons have been included to help you with visual cues about what is coming up next so that you can be prepared and have materials ready.

	Typical responses, previous class input
	Notes and tips for the facilitator
	Warning about a particular challenge that may arise during the presentation
	Show visuals on an overhead or LCD projector
	Use a flip chart
	Timed activity
	Handouts

UNIT 1
Program Introduction
Total Time: 20 minutes

Step 1: Participants arrive. *(10 minutes)*

Step 2: Discuss *What Do You See?* visual. *(2 minutes)*

Step 3: Debrief candy choices. *(1 minute)*

Step 4: *Who are You? (1 minute)*

Step 5: Handwriting exercise. *(4 minutes)*

Step 6: Introduce type preferences and agenda. *(2 minutes)*

Step 1: Participants arrive. (10 minutes)

As people arrive: Project the *What Do You See?* visual (V-1) so that students can see it as soon as they enter the room, but do not call attention to it.

"In our experience, this double image was rarely familiar, and it really got exchanges going, sometimes even arguments! If you think the image is 'worn out' choose another double image and use the exercise we provided as an example."

Point out the bowl with candy and the sign asking them to take just one piece.

Have music on and encourage people to choose other music from CDs you have brought.

Encourage people to look at any posted materials and books you have provided if they so wish.

These activities create a nonschool atmosphere and give teens something to do and a way to engage with each other.

Step 2: Discuss *What Do You See?* visual. (2 minutes)

Without any introduction, call attention to the visual.

"Let's talk about the picture. What do you see? What are we looking at?"

Then say nothing more.

Let participants discuss freely and show each other the two ways to see the picture. If everyone who speaks sees it the same way, ask who sees something different.

Record some of the comments people make.

After most in the group have seen the picture both ways, say the following:

"Once you see things in a certain way, it can be hard to change your perspective and see them another way. It can, however, be done with some effort. Personality type, what we are going to talk about today, is similar to this exercise: You see one way first but, with time, you can learn to see the other way. For example, you may see your parents concern about where you are as a lack of trust. But, eventually, you realize they are just worried. You may see a teacher as a real jerk, but someone else likes her and, eventually, you see why."

Step 3: Debrief candy choices. (1 minute)

With lots of energy, ask everyone to stand up.

> *"OK, I'd like the people who chose peppermint to move to the left of the room here and those who chose butterscotch to move to the right.*
>
> *Based on your choice of candy, we have two types here. The butterscotches and the peppermints."*

Do the following in your own style—you just need to exaggerate enough to make the point of how silly it looks when you discriminate because of small differences.

Say to those who chose peppermint, with exaggeration:

> *"What do you think of these butterscotches? Do they look a little weird, maybe? Do you think you can trust them? Maybe their taste isn't that great?"*

Then say to those who chose butterscotch:

> *"Hmm, butterscotches, I'm not so sure about those peppermints! They seem a little self-important. I mean, they took peppermint and all. I'm not sure I would want to be with people who chose peppermint."*

When participants start to smile or look confused at the absurdity of your suggestions, say:

> *"Obviously, what I'm saying is ridiculous. We don't get suspicious or look down on people because they chose butterscotch or peppermint. They're not inferior or untrustworthy. They just made a different choice. They preferred a different candy. And choices like this may change from day to day."*

Tell them they can have all the candy they want now.

 Have people remain standing, gathering around the screen if they wish.

4

Step 4: *Who Are You?* (1 minute)

"We have already seen two examples of preferences, differences in the way people see things and the choices they make. When you chose candy you thought a bit about it—peppermint or butter-scotch—then made a conscious choice. In looking at the **What Do You See?** *picture, you didn't make a choice. What you saw first came automatically. Today we are looking at things we do automatically—inborn preferences. Let's look first at other things that make us who we are."*

Put up the visual V-2, *Who Are You?*

"What kind of things do you see acting on you from the outside?"

Write the answers in the categories on an overhead projector, or type them into your computer to display through the LCD projector, or write them on an easel large enough for participants to read. Try to steer them toward specific words, not general terms like family or culture.

"These are things that start to act on you as soon as you are born. But personality type is one of the things we believe is inborn."

Circle "personality type" inside the head of the person depicted on V-2.

"These outside things are easier to see than inside preferences. But today we will take some of these inner preferences out and examine them. You may even begin to learn to recognize preferences in yourself and other people."

Ask participants to sit down, and then pass out paper and pencils.

Step 5: Handwriting Exercise (4 minutes)

"OK, just take a piece of paper and write your name—just as you normally do. Don't worry, it won't be collected. What is this experience like for you?"

Fine, normal, no big deal, automatic, didn't think about it.

"Now write your name with the other hand. What is this experience like for you? Different? How? I hear some groans and moans."

Slow, hard! Looks awful, took so long, I could do it but only if I concentrated.

"We can see from this exercise that an inborn preference for left- or right-handedness is similar to inborn preferences for type. When you use your preferred hand, it is easy; you are used to it and you don't even have to think. When you use your nonpreferred hand, the results aren't as good; it's uncomfortable and it takes hard work, and it takes more energy, etc.

When we are allowed to write with our preferred hand from childhood, we feel comfortable and it becomes easy for us. In the same way, when we are allowed to be who we are and use our natural preferences, we feel comfortable and energized.

The hand a person feels comfortable with is probably their preferred hand; but you should not make that assumption. Sometimes people use their nonpreferred hand because of an injury, because most tools such as scissors are made for 'righties,' because of an awkward or confined space that prohibits the other hand from freely moving, or for some other reasons. You cannot assume that the person hammering with their left hand is left-handed. A person may be forced to use their opposite hand by the situation or may have developed the ability to use it by choice."

"Has anyone ever broken their writing arm? What happened?"

I could use the other hand when I had to but it felt awkward. It was tiring. But I got used to it—it got better.

"In just the same way, when we are forced to act in ways that don't honor our preferences, we can do it but it can feel stressed and uncomfortable. Families and teachers, even friends, can force us to use nonpreferences. They can even tell us our preferences are wrong. This criticism can make us feel uncomfortable or force us to work too hard at what is not natural for us. "

Give your examples of pressure to behave in certain ways in school or social situations.

Reinforce your point by asking people to fold their arms together in front of their chest.

After they have done it in their unconsciously preferred manner, ask them to do it the other way.

"This is another example of how both ways can be right but how one way may feel less natural. If arm-folding were a key part of life, and you were constantly forced to do it the nonpreferred way, it might make you uncomfortable and even stressed under certain circumstances."

Step 6: Introduce type preferences and agenda. (2 minutes)

Put up V-3, *The Four MBTI® Preference Pairs.*

"Now, let's look at type preferences. As you can see, there are four pairs of preferences. When you have one preference from each pair, you see a four letter type. So there are sixteen possible types. When you identify a type that you believe describes you, this is only an approximate description. It doesn't mean you are exactly like anyone else of that type.

Type is not meant to put people in categories or boxes. It isn't meant to limit choices of experiences or jobs or friends, or anything, In fact, for young people in particular, you will want to try lots of experiences to see which best fits your preferences.

Today you will be giving some thought to what type you might be. But that is only for your own use and only with one objective—to understand yourself and other people better."

Review the agenda posted on the wall.

At this point, you should introduce some of the history of the Indicator. A brief history is provided here, but you may wish to create your own version of MBTI history, depending on your style and your audience.

We suggest an abbreviated version of the history of type, because, as noted earlier, experience has shown that it is important to move quickly during the initial stages of the presentation.

If you find that you need a more in-depth version, Katharine Myers, a trustee of the Myers and Briggs Foundation, has created one for this program that can be found on the Resources CD-ROM as a participant material (PM-5). This longer history can be excerpted, used as a foundation for your history, or reproduced and passed out to students at the end of the program. The important point is to tell the history like a story and *not* like a lecture. Since lectures or long speeches will diffuse the energy that has been built to this point, be aware of how you present this information.

Young people may want to hear that Isabel was homeschooled and that her boyfriend was different from her family. The story you tell can be designed for your particular audience. For example: an historical or biographical bent would cover dates and people, a career development slant would look at how Isabel's early interest in people became a career. You may find yourself sprinkling some of the biographical and historical information throughout the workshop but, at this point in the program, keep the energy high by being brief.

 Biographical information about Isabel and Katharine has had additional side benefits when included in the history of the Indicator. One year, this history helped a student prepare for the role of Isabel Myers as a member of a panel with other historical figures such as Plato, Descartes, and Piaget.

"These ideas about type come from the concepts developed in the 1920s by a Swiss psychiatrist named Carl G. Jung. During the 1940s, two Americans, Katharine Cook Briggs and her daughter Isabel Briggs Myers, explored Jung's ideas while they were developing their own theories about psychological type. Their goal was to make Jung's ideas usable by people who weren't psychiatrists or psychologists. They developed the first version of the questionnaire you took before you came to this workshop, the Myers-Briggs Type Indicator instrument, which is now the most used personality instrument in the world.

The good news is that it does not tell you what you should be, it only alerts you to your natural preferences. Every preference, thus every type, is equally valuable. There are no 'right' or 'wrong' types; there are just different types."

If you haven't been introduced by someone at the beginning of the workshop, take a few minutes to introduce yourself, emphasizing how you have used the program or worked with teens.

"Are there any questions at this point? If you think of one later, just ask it during the session or, if you prefer, ask me at a break.

Now we are going to begin observing some personality type differences."

UNIT 2
Extraversion (E) and Introversion (I)
Total Time: 30 minutes

Step 1: Conduct the fishbowl exercise: *Grading for Participation. (15 minutes)*

Step 2: Debrief the fishbowl exercise. *(5 minutes)*

Step 3: Introduce the E–I preferences. *(5 minutes)*

Step 4: Ask participants to complete worksheets. *(5 minutes)*

1

Step 1: Conduct fishbowl exercise: *Grading for Participation.* (15 min)

"We will now do an exercise to explore one of the ways in which people are different. Here are some groups we have formed. I would like to ask these people to step outside for a few minutes while we set up the exercise."

 You have already selected the students for these two groups (page 59), but don't tell them they are divided by type. If necessary, have an adult monitor go with them when they leave the room.

Assemble those who remain in the room.

 Put up the flip chart with this question on it: *The teachers of your school are proposing to have 25 percent of your grade based on class participation. What is your response to this idea?*

"This is the question I am going to ask each group to discuss. As they discuss it, you have a critical role in this exercise as observers. As they discuss the issues, I would like you to look for some of these things:

- *Noise level*

- *Length of pause between two people speaking*

- *Interruptions*

- *More than one person talking at one time*

- *Side conversations with each other or the audience*

- *Body language (such as gesturing to use the marker, telling someone 'shh,' or hands at side or on lap)*

Besides observing each group, notice also how the groups differ on these points. It is very important that you NOT interact with the groups in any way."

Bring the Introverts back in and ask them to stand in a group in front of the class.

Have the group members who were not divided out stand and gather around them to watch but not to interact.

 Show the Introverts the flip chart with the question and give them 5 minutes to discuss.

At the end of 5 minutes, ask the group members to stop, thank them, and give the observers a few moments to make notes. Make your own notes to share later as appropriate.

Explain to those in the first group that the next group will discuss the question, and the first group should observe the interactions.

Invite the Extraverts in and repeat the process.

Thank both groups and congratulate them on their efforts.

2

Step 2: Debrief the fishbowl exercise. (5 minutes)

"I'd like to ask the observers to share what they noticed about one group or the other. Please comment on two things: how people acted in the group and also how each group reacted to the idea of their grade being based on participation."

Note comments about the Extravert group on one flip chart and the Introvert group on another but do not label them yet.

Now ask members of the E and I groups to share their experiences. What was easy and what was difficult and why?

 Reinforce the idea that there are no right or wrong answers or behaviors.

 Comments about Introverted behaviors may include the following:

- Speak one at a time
- May pause up to a count of five between time one person stops and other begins
- Rarely initiate interaction with audience but may respond when spoken to
- Don't interrupt much

Comments about Extraverted behavior may include the following:

- Are distracting and chatty while waiting in the hall
- Are in the middle of conversations when entering the room
- Try to engage with the audience
- May have two conversations at once
- May pause only one second before speaking
- May interrupt each other

"As we look at these two flip charts, we can see that some people get energy from interacting with others in a group and look forward to getting credit for participation. These people may have a preference for Extraversion."

Write Extraversion on the flip chart.

"Those who seem to get less energy and who are less inclined to participate may have a preference for Introversion."

Write Introversion on the other flip chart.

"Let's take a closer look at these two preferences."

My parents get on to me about waiting to the last minute to begin my school projects, but I don't like to start until I feel I have gathered all the information that's out there.

Step 3: Introduce the E–I preferences. (5 minutes)

"Extraversion and Introversion are words we often use in conversation but in terms of psychological type, their meaning is a little different. Carl Jung used these terms in a way true to their Latin roots— extraversion as 'turning outward' and introversion as 'turning inward.' They do not mean, as many people think, that Extraverts are social or talkative or that Introverts are unsocial or shy.

E and I are about energy and the direction of attention. Extraversion is being energized by contact with the outside world; looking to interact with it. People who prefer Extraversion lose some energy from too much time alone. Introversion is being energized by the inner world. Foe people who prefer Introversion, energy is decreased by too much contact with the outer world. So Extraversion is not just talking and socializing, and Introversion is not merely being quiet and spending time alone."

Using visuals V-6A through V-6G, describe the Extraverted and Introverted preferences. (You may use your own explanations or refer to the scripted comments for the visuals starting on page 176.)

Comment on how the illustrations reflect Extraversion and Introversion.

Give examples from other classes and your own experience.

Encourage participants to give examples of their own and to ask questions.

Use cartoons as appropriate to amplify the meaning of these preferences.

Show V-6G and quickly summarize the two preferences. Point to the character at the bottom and say the following:

"This fellow is a reminder that, even though we prefer one preference, we are capable of using the other preference. That nonpreferred way is somewhere inside and there will be times when you will need to reach for and use this preference.

And down at the bottom are some reminders that people who prefer each preference still need the people of the opposite preference. Extraverts need Introverts to slow them down and help them focus. Introverts need Extraverts to help get their ideas out into the world.

E and I also refer to how people do their initial processing of information. The Extravert, for example, does his or her best thinking in the external world. Thus, you may find a person who prefers Extraversion will write more easily after they have 'talked through' a subject. You may also see Extraverts talking to themselves when they are thinking because they are trying to find their ideas. Someone with a preference for Introversion might have an easier time talking the topic out after thinking it through. They may find that talking to others in the early stages makes it more difficult to find the ideas they want to use. Many of the recommendations about how to do homework say to work alone, a method which may favor the preference for Introversion.

It also explains why doing homework alone right after school may not be effective for all students.

Which of these two preferences do you think our society in general approves of most?"

Let the students come to their own conclusions. Ask them for examples to support what they say. The answer is generally that Extraversion is favored. (Keep current with type research on U.S. population.)

"Which of the two preferences are favored in this group's environment (school, youth group, etc.)?"

The answer will depend on the group but allow participants to discuss the issue and give examples.

"This bias toward one preference in your (group, school, etc.) might mean you have to learn to use your nonpreferred approach, and that might not be easy for you. However, uncomfortable does NOT equate with incapable. It may not feel natural to express Extraversion when you prefer Introversion, or vice versa, but you can practice using your least-preferred approach and learn to use it when needed.

It is good to note that when someone is forced to use their nonpreferred approach over a long period of time (as opposed to when they have developed that ability deliberately), they may become stressed if they do not find ways to also use their preferred approach some of the time."

Use the following questions posted on a flip chart to stimulate discussion.

How does your E–I preference affect how you use your free time after school or on weekends?

How might E–I differences cause misunderstandings or bad feelings?

Step 4: Ask participants to complete worksheets. (5 minutes)

Put up visuals *First Guess Type* (V-4) and *Who Influences You?* (V-5).

Pass out the worksheets entitled *First Guess Type* (PM-1) and *Who Influences You?* (PM-2).

Ask the participants to immediately put their names on both sheets, as it is easy for them to get mixed up.

Using V-4, walk through how to complete the *First Guess Type* worksheet (PM-1).

"However, you may not feel ready to make a first guess, and that is not unusual. Just leave it blank and you may at some later time decide you feel ready to fill it in."

Now ask participants to look at the *Who Influences You?* worksheet (PM-2).

"When you begin to think about what your own preferences might be, you sometimes see how others may influence you. For example, your best friend seems to prefer Extraversion and always wants to be out and about and he enjoys asking people over to his place and thinks big groups are better than groups of two or three. As a result, you may feel that's the right way to be and begin to act like you prefer Extraversion, even though in your heart you feel more like you prefer Introversion. Or, if people in your family prefer Introversion and frequently arrange for quiet and time alone, it may seem that this is the only way to be because it is so familiar. This worksheet will help us sort out these influences. It may also explain some ways in which you differ from other people in how you are energized.

Remember that as you look at influences on your preferences, you are making some educated guesses about what might be the preferences of other people in your world. Remember that we can't type other people: these are only observations about how people seem to you."

This is the first time that participants have to think about the concept of who is influencing their type. Provide VERY specific examples in each area (mix up examples from family, teachers, and friends). Without examples, participants may not fully explore the possibilities of where type influences come from.

 You want to set a tone that these worksheets are important and should be given some careful thought. Do this by keeping the room quiet and waiting until most of the class is no longer working before moving on.

Encourage people to share their examples if they have any.

Walk around as people work and see if anyone needs assistance.

"You will probably not fill in every section of this worksheet. It is just there to record any thoughts about who might be influencing you to be one type or another. We will be looking at E and I again later in the workshop."

Summarize the E–I unit.

- We are talking about what you prefer to do, not what you can do.

- We all use both preferences. What you use naturally is your preferred approach. But you can use the other if it is needed at a given moment.

- When you observe others extraverting or introverting, it doesn't necessarily mean that it is what they prefer. It is just the preference they are using at that moment. This is why it is dangerous to decide someone else's type based on what you see.

Call a break of 10 minutes and be sure it goes no longer than 15 minutes.

 Always stay in the room during the breaks and make yourself available for students to approach you with questions or concerns.

-- 15 MINUTE BREAK --

UNIT 3
Sensing (S) and Intuition (N)
Total Time: 30 minutes

Step 1: Conduct the candle exercise (or alternate). *(5 minutes)*

Step 2: Introduce the S–N preferences. *(5 minutes)*

Step 3: Ask participants to complete worksheets. *(5 minutes)*

Step 4: Conduct the poster exercise. *(10 minutes)*

Step 5: Summarize the poster exercise. *(5 minutes)*

Step 1: Conduct the candle exercise (or alternate). (5 minutes)

Place the candle in the holder on a table in front of the class and light it. Wait a few seconds. Or use an alternate exercise if fire regulations prohibit the use of an open flame.

"Tell me about the candle. Tell me some things that you see and the ideas that come into your mind as you're looking at it."

Note on a flip chart the words participants use.

When you have 10 or 12 words on the flip chart, blow out the candle and turn to the flip chart.

"We seem to have two different kinds of information here; some words and phrases give actual details, like 'red,' 'made of wax,' 'gives off light,' and 'the wick is black and about a quarter inch high' (use examples from the flip chart for your group). Other words and phrases are general ideas such as 'hope,' 'cozy,' 'peace,' and 'uncertain' (again, use the words from your own group). These differences reflect the next set of preferences, called Sensing and Intuition."

2

Step 2: Introduce the S–N preferences. (5 minutes)

"Sensing and Intuition refer to the type of information that catches one's interest. This is especially important in learning because different students exposed to the same information are likely to retain different parts of that information, based on their preference in this pair.

The differences in this pair can be hard to understand. Basically, those who prefer Sensing see the details of what is there. Those who prefer Intuition see associations, interpretations, or possibilities sparked by what is there.

Both preferences are used by everyone depending on the type of information that needs to be processed or understood. For example, Sensing is used to name the specific parts of a skeleton; to put a decimal point in the right place; to add, subtract, multiply, or divide; to punctuate and spell without mistakes; to add details such as colors, place, and size in writing, describe real events with accuracy; or to verify facts in current events and history. Intuition is used to invent characters and adventures in creative writing; to make up metaphors; to find the theme of a novel; to interpret a poem; to speculate about what could have happened or may happen in history; and to pose theories about anything from math and science to social studies or philosophy."

Give examples from other classes and your own experience.

 Show the visuals V-7A through V-7G and quickly summarize the two preferences. (You may use your own explanations or refer to the scripted comments for the visuals, pages 177–178.)

Point to the character near the bottom of the V-7G and say:

"You can see an example here of how, when we have to, we can use our nonpreferred way. Hopefully, it will not take a broken bone to help you realize that you can learn to bring out your nonpreferred way when it is desired or needed for a situation."

"At the bottom of the visual are some reminders that regardless of which preference you have, you will need the perspective of people with the opposite preference."

Read out loud the last lines on the visual.

"What are some examples of how these differences show up in your life?"

Show cartoons that illustrate the difference between Sensing and Intuition if you have them.

Don't use cartoons that make one preference look better than the other.

"Which of these two preferences do you think our society in general approves of most? What are some examples of how one preference seems to be favored?"

Usually people will decide Sensing is favored.

"Now let's think for a minute about which of the two preferences are favored in your own environment (school, youth group, etc.). What do you think?"

The answer will depend on the group but allow them to discuss and give examples.

"Actually, according to study data collected about type, about 75% of people in the U.S. choose Sensing on the Indicator."

Of the current samples, 73.3% prefer Sensing and 26.7% prefer Intuition. (Myers et al. 1998.)

"This may explain some things. The Sensing preference allows us to access details and how-to information. Think of the specific details we use: phone numbers, birth dates, addresses, locker combinations, song lyrics, movie and bus schedules. We use Sensing to use an ATM machine. We would use Sensing to pay attention to the detailed instructions that come with a video camera or a computer.

The Intuitive preference allows us to see more than one meaning. Think of the letter X. It is a letter in the alphabet but sometimes it means 'multiply' and for Valentines Day it could mean 'kiss.' The yin-yang symbol can be said to mean balance or opposites and more. And, remember the electronic equipment we just mentioned when discussing Sensing? With Intuition, we can imagine computer uses that haven't been invented yet.

Remember, you CAN use both preferences. You may feel uncomfortable using your nonpreferred approach, but you are capable of using it when you need to. However, if forced to use your nonpreferred over a long period of time, you may become stressed."

It bothers me when my friends are not getting along with each other. I find myself wanting to help people reconcile their interpersonal issues before I can concentrate on my studies.

3

Step 3: Ask participants to complete the worksheets. (5 minutes)

Direct participants' attention to the worksheets entitled *First Guess Type* (PM-1) *and Who Influences You?* (PM-2).

Show visuals V-4 and V-5 again.

"Take out your First Guess Type worksheet again. Remember what I said when you did this worksheet for Extraversion and Introversion. These sheets are here to help make a first guess if you are ready. But it is certainly OK not to make a first guess now if it's not comfortable. Remember also that no one sees these sheets and you can take a guess now and change it later. You do not need to commit to one choice or the other."

Now ask participants to turn to the *Who Influences You?* worksheet.

"Just as with E and I, when you begin to think about what your own preferences might be, you sometimes see how others may influence you. So for example, if your parent has preferences for Sensing and is always quizzing you about exact facts or dismissing your ideas about what could be, you may feel you should act like you prefer Sensing, even though in your heart you are more interested in possibilities and associations.

Or if you feel that you have a preference for Sensing, but a teacher constantly uses your metaphors and connections as examples of how to go deeper into a topic, then Intuition may seem like the best preference, since you are constantly praised for it. This worksheet helps us sort out these influences. It may also explain some ways in which you differ from other people in how you take in information: by dealing with specific details or by looking at the general ideas."

Probe to see that everyone understands these examples because teens tend not to ask if they don't get something.

Once again, this is a tough concept. Provide VERY specific examples in each area (family, teachers, and friends).

Encourage people to share their own examples if they have them.

Walk around to see if anyone needs assistance.

"Remember, you will probably not fill in every section of this worksheet. It is just there to record any thoughts about who might influence you to be one type or another. We will be looking at S and N again later in the workshop.

Now we are now going to look at how to apply your knowledge of Sensing and Intuition in real life. This is a particularly important type preference pair in school because it relates to the way you like to take in and share information, what kind of information you like to learn, and what kind of information teachers ask for."

Step 4: Conduct the poster exercise. (10 minutes)

"I'd like you now to divide into Sensing and Intuition groups, based on the first guess you just made."

If there are more than 5 or 6 in one group, divide the groups again into smaller groups.

"You do not have to be absolutely sure which you prefer. Just go to the group that you feel is more likely yours. If you are really uncertain, you can act as an observer. But if you do that, you cannot interact with the groups at all."

 You will have to enforce this rule. People tend to forget. If observers DO participate, it dilutes the effect of the exercise.

Give each group flip-chart paper and markers, and tell them to write down what their group says. Uncover or hang up the poster you have chosen to use for this exercise.

"Now here is what I want you to do. Tell us about the poster."

 Allow about 5 minutes for the groups to work.

 If you see someone very frustrated in one group, suggest that they try a group of the other preference to see if it suits them better.

Ask each group to present what they put on their flip-chart paper.

5
Step 5: Summarize the poster exercise. (5 minutes)

"Wow. You can see that there are clearly different kinds of information here. Now, which group's words would best allow you to find the poster in a store?"

 The answer is, of course, Sensing, because it actually describes what is on the poster.

"Which group's words would convey the meaning or overall impression of the poster?"

Wait for response of Intuition.

"So, different information can accomplish different things. Now let's look at how understanding these Sensing and Intuitive preferences can help you be successful in writing papers or answering essay questions in class.

Using this poster as an example, let's consider various scenarios that might happen in a classroom.

Students who prefer Intuition may hear the teacher say, 'You need more detail about your description of the posters. What did you see in the poster that made you use that word?'

Students who prefer Sensing may hear the teachers say, 'These are just facts that you wrote down for your description. But what does it mean? What does it symbolize? I need you to tell me what the words may symbolize.'"

Each student needs to tell the whole story—both the details and the meaning. The associations will come easily to Ns and they must add facts. The facts will come easier to Ss and they must add associations.

Most often for school situations, you will need to actively use both Sensing and Intuition by doing what is easiest for you first and then using the other preference for either the details or the associations.

One way to help you to do this is to get help from someone with the opposite preference. If you prefer Sensing, a person who prefers Intuition can help identify meanings. If you prefer Intuition, then a person who prefers Sensing can help you identify the facts."

UNIT 4
Thinking (T) and Feeling (F)
Total Time: 30 minutes

Step 1: Conduct the fishbowl exercise: *Who Stays Home?* *(10 minutes)*

Step 2: Debrief the fishbowl exercise. *(10 minutes)*

Step 3: Introduce the T–F preferences. *(5 minutes)*

Step 4: Ask participants to complete worksheets. *(5 minutes)*

Step 1: Run the fishbowl exercise: Who Stays Home? (10 minutes)

"We have been looking at how people take in information and what kind of information grabs their attention. Now we are going to look at how people make decisions with that information."

Read the names for the fishbowl groups but do not tell participants how they were chosen.

Ask both groups to go out of the room and, if necessary or available, send an adult monitor with them.

Read the *scenario* for *Who Stays Home?* on page 101 and review the instructions for the discussion.

If participants object that this scenario would not happen or that they need more information, tell them that "for the sake of the exercise, this is the situation we are going to work with."

"For those of you who are in neither group, you have a critical role in this exercise as observers. I have just read the dilemma that each group will be asked to discuss. As they discuss possible solutions, I would like you to note some of the following:

- *How do individuals label or describe someone else's ideas?*

- *Are ideas phrased as commands or questions?*

- *What factors does each group look at in deciding?*

- *Body language such as dismissive hand gestures or grimaces that show the decision is difficult.*

Please, DO NOT interact with the people in the fishbowl."

Note to Facilitator: The point of this exercise is that there are more people in the group in the Disney scenario than can be accommodated. Fill in the exact numbers so that they fit the group you are facilitating. Where the original has 22, insert the real number in your group. Where the original has 18, put in 4 fewer than the real number in your group.

"Good news! An eccentric local millionaire has selected this group at random to go on a free three-day trip to Disney World. In making this grant, the millionaire was most understanding and generous. If you are working, she will provide someone to take your place while you are gone and will pay the salary. She will pay you any salary you may lose while on the trip. She will provide you with funds for any additions to your wardrobe and any camera or recording equipment you need for this once-in-a-lifetime experience.

There is one problem, however. She was misinformed about the size of your group. Her invitation covers expenses for only 18 (____) students. Since there are 22 (____) students in this group, class, four of you will not be able to go. Additional money won't help because all the reservations and activities have been planned for only 18 (____) students. You have all been members of the group for the same amount of time. Grades are not to be taken into consideration. Everyone is available to go and wants to go.

Your group has been chosen to make the decision. Assume that
- *you have all been members of the group the same amount of time,*
- *grades are not a factor, and*
- *your group must tell the four students who won't go."*

Bring the Feeling group back in while the Thinking group waits outside.

Read the scenario and ask the Feeling group to discuss the situation and possible solutions.

It is very important during these discussions to enforce the conditions in the assignment regarding "everyone wants to go" and "you have belonged to the group for the same amount of time." Groups tend to forget these constraints. Do not let them get away from making a decision on the difficult issue by brainstorming solutions that make it possible for all to go.

Make your own observations to help you debrief.

 When 5 minutes are up, thank them for a good job and have them sit down.

Allow a few minutes for observers to jot down notes without any discussion.

Now ask the Thinking group to return to the room.

Read the scenario and ask the Thinking group to discuss the situation and possible solutions.

 When the 5 minutes are up, thank them, ask them to sit down, and allow time for observers to jot down notes.

Learning about type has helped me
understand my parents a better. We are able
to work through problems a little easier.

Step 2: Debrief the fishbowl exercise. (10 minutes)

"Let's look for a minute at differences in the way these groups worked with the dilemma.

What differences did you see in the way the Thinking and Feeling groups discussed the scenario?

What criteria did each group look at to make the decision?

How were the actual decisions different?

What did the process look like to outside observers?

How did it feel to be in one of these groups?"

 Here are some common responses:

- Both Thinking types and Feeling types may suggest drawing straws or names out of a hat, but their rationales will differ. The Thinking perspective sees this as objective and may even use the word "probability." The Feeling perspective will want to avoid being personally responsible for excluding someone.

- To be fair, Thinking types may suggest using factors like birth date, height, or shoe size. Thinking types may also make comments such as "that's silly" or "how dumb is that" when they hear the solutions from the Feeling types group. They may ask who decides the standard or criteria that will be used to determine what's best.

- Feeling types may suggest playing a game and losers stay home, or having a sleepover and the first to fall asleep stays home, or writing essays and the group chooses the authors of the best ones to go.

Step 3: Introduce the T–F preferences. (5 minutes)

"It is important to remember that the words Thinking and Feeling can be misunderstood, since Thinking types definitely feel and Feeling types do think. Both preferences use a rational and deliberate way of making decisions. Feeling does not mean emotional. Thinking does not mean intelligent. Keep that in mind as we look at these preferences."

Refer to V-8A through V-8G and review the descriptions of the T and F preferences quickly.

"I want to emphasize here that Thinking and Feeling refer to the way in which we make decisions, not necessarily what we decide. They refer to what criteria we look at first, even though we may use both preferences before we make the final decision. Sometimes two people with the opposite preferences can come to the same decision but for different reasons.

These preferences are often seen as related to gender, because in statistical analyses more males choose T and more females choose F. This may be because of the cultural norms that influence us, so that males are programmed to see themselves as Thinking types and females are programmed to see themselves as Feeling types. However, these are considered preferences, and not gender differences. Many males prefer a Feeling approach and many females prefer a Thinking approach.

Because of this social bias, males who prefer Feeling and females who prefer Thinking often feel they don't fit in. Feeling males may be seen as too sensitive and Thinking females as too aggressive."

Be alert to comments that reflect either gender conditioning or the idea that Feeling is the same as emotions or that Thinking is the same as intelligence. Correct these misunderstandings whenever they appear and reconfirm the actual definitions of Thinking and Feeling when necessary.

"Sometimes differences between people on these two preferences can create difficulties because they can strike at deeply held values. For example, what happens if a student breaks a rule? A teacher with a Feeling preference might want to give the student another chance, citing unusual circumstances. A teacher with a Thinking preference, on the other hand, might feel that the rule should be upheld, to be fair to everyone. One teacher may appear unfair and the other may appear uncaring."

Give examples about young people from other classes and your own experience.

Point to V-8G and review the descriptors of each preference.

"Remember, once again, that we can all use both preferences: Thinking and Feeling. And that Feeling types need Thinking types and vice versa.

Can someone give an example of how Thinking and Feeling show up in this group (or class)?"

Use cartoons as appropriate to amplify the meaning of these preferences.

"Which of these two preferences do you think our society in general approves of most? Most groups will conclude that it is Thinking. Modern western societies tend to validate the Thinking preference more, evident in our emphasis on a cause and effect approach to analysis of most topics."

Give more examples, if necessary, from everyday life.

"This bias toward one preference in your environment might be causing you to use a nonpreferred approach. While any person can use both preferences, you are more comfortable with your preferred way. If forced to use your nonpreferred approach over a long period of time, you may become stressed. We'll look at this in just a minute when we do the Who Influences You? worksheet."

Step 4: Ask participants to complete worksheets. (5 minutes)

Ask participants to take out their two worksheets *First Guess Type* (PM-1) and *Who Influences You?* (PM-2).

Show the visuals (V-4 and V-5) of those worksheets.

"Take a few minutes now to make a first guess on this preference pair. Remember that it is OK not to make a first guess now if you are not comfortable with either of the choices at this time.

You have already looked at how other people may be influencing you to be one preference, even if your real preference is the opposite. With Thinking and Feeling, there is especially pressure to prefer the 'right' preference for your gender, even though such a thing does not exist. In this pair, for example, a woman who looks first at logic may hear from her family that she is cold and unfeeling. This may encourage her to believe she should prefer Feeling—that her Thinking preference is somehow 'wrong.' And she may start to demonstrate a Feeling approach to situations, even though it goes against her natural preference.

A man who prefers Feeling may be told that he is not 'macho' enough or he is too sensitive. This feedback, combined with gender expectations, can create a lot of stress and may pressure a male with preferences for Feeling to prefer Thinking.

As we know, you cannot force a preference; it is natural. So this kind of 'pretending' even when it is unconscious, can create enormous stress over time."

Remember to probe to see that participants understand these examples because teens tend not to ask if they don't get something.

"Does anyone have other examples of how people might be pressured by their environment to go against their Feeling or Thinking preference?

OK, take a few minutes to think about this and jot down any notes about influences you may feel in this area. Remember, these notes are only for you and will not be shown to anyone else."

Walk around as they work and help anyone who seems puzzled.

"A little later you will have a chance to look at how to apply your knowledge of Thinking and Feeling in real life.

Next we are going to look at the last pair of preferences, which are important and can have an enormous impact on how people interact with one another. These concern how we organize our lives in the outside world."

Call a break of 10 minutes and be sure it goes no longer than 15 minutes.

 Always stay in the room during the breaks and make yourself available for students to approach you with questions or concern.

-- 15 MINUTE BREAK --

UNIT 5
Judging (J) and Perceiving (P)

Total Time: 35 minutes

Step 1: Present the skit: *The Paper Is Due!* *(10 minutes)*

Step 2: Debrief the skit. *(5 minutes)*

Step 3: Introduce the J–P preferences. *(5 minutes)*

Step 4: Ask participants to complete worksheets. *(5 minutes)*

Step 5: Conduct application exercise: "The Line-Up." *(10 minutes)*

Step 1: Present the skit: *The Paper Is Due!* (10 minutes)

"We are going to start exploring the final set of preferences through the presentation of a skit or 'slice of life.' This may look somewhat familiar."

Ask the participants who will present the skit to sit in chairs up front and encourage the rest of the class to gather round to observe the skit closely, taking notes if they wish.

The mood should be fun but don't let actors get silly. DO NOT allow the "audience" to make comments to the actors.

Leader's Guide *The Paper Is Due!* (RM-3) by Leann Bertram

This skit was created to illustrate that the Judging and Perceiving attitudes are two different but equally valuable and competent ways to complete a task. The skit also provides an opportunity to explain the difference between procrastination and the preference for perceiving.

The skit has two people and a number of scenes. In each scene both characters read from a dialogue sheet and use props as noted.

Props

- Two telephones.
- One set of student supplies: calendar or date book, index cards, assignment book.
- Two scripts. (The facilitator will need to prepare the scripts by pasting the 18 pages on both sides of 8 1/2 x 11 oak tag. The bold letters describing how much time is left for the assignment should be on one side for the audience to read. The script is pasted onto the flip side.)
- Two "final papers" with appropriate grades. (These should also be pasted onto oak tag with the name of the paper on one side and the final grade and the MBTI type on the other side.)

Process

The skit concerns two students completing a report during a four-week period. Each actor has props and a set of dialogue sheets including a report cover with the final grade of A+. The actors hold up one dialogue sheet at a time so the audience can read the bold print while they read from the back side where the script is printed. This allows the audience to see time passing as the actors say their lines.

Coach the actors beforehand to make it fun and keep it light. Although surprise is OK, they should not demonstrate anger or other emotions. Tell them to avoid loud, high pitched voices, clenched jaws and fists, etc. If emotions take over, the dialogue has left the type dichotomy we are trying to demonstrate.

Facilitator Notes

The two students are in the process of completing a paper. Note where in the process each student has the energy to limit the focus, decide the topic, and complete the task. Notice that one student decides, or comes to closure and begins to work towards completion, nearer the time the assignment is given. The other maintains a broad and inclusive focus examining many topics and doesn't make a final selection until the due date is near. It is important to note that this student does not *procrastinate* (put off work) but rather spontaneously examines many alternatives as the work is completed. Both curiosity and spontaneity are part of a preferred work process.

For more information about procrastination and MBTI preferences, please see *Procrastination: Using Psychological Type Concepts to Help Students* by Judith Provost.

"I saw lots of smiles and knowing nods during the skit. You have probably known—or even been—the people in this situation. It is tempting to just label the way these students were acting. But let's take a deeper look at how their approaches reflect differences in type."

If you have written the following questions on a flip chart, show them now and ask them one at a time. Remember that they do not yet know the terms Judging and Perceiving so just refer to the role-players by their real names.

"How were the students different in terms of when they began to focus on the due date?"

These points will probably come out: J (use name of participant) began to focus right away; P (use name of participant) began to focus later.

"Where in the process did they 'trade off' their play time for work time in order get the paper done on time?"

These points will probably come out: J gave up play to work more in the beginning, while P had time to play early on but had to really buckle down near the due date.

"What characteristics contribute to each student's success?"

These points will probably come out: J is focused, sticks to plan, budgets his time. P is flexible, open to new ideas, energized by nearness of due date, doesn't panic.

"What are some problems each approach could create for the student?"

Js: Might miss some play opportunities; original idea less likely to evolve (carved in stone); gets called "bossy"; find it more difficult to do something else if assignment changes.

Ps: May be seen as disorganized; unexpected obstacles could throw off tight timing; may have problems with teammates if they are working on a group project.

 Watch for negative adjectives used to describe either work style so you can address them when you introduce the preferences in the next step. Perceiving types in particular are often described negatively as unmotivated, uncaring, or lazy. Judging types may be called rigid, uptight, or too serious.

I feel overwhelmed when my teachers give too many details. It helps me to get a big picture first; then the detail information makes more sense.

3

Step 3: Introduce the J–P preferences. (5 minutes)

"These are preferences for managing our lives in the outside world. In other words, some people prefer, in the outer world, to gather information (using either Sensing or Intuition). Others prefer, when in the outer world, to make decisions (using either Thinking or Feeling). This results in distinctive ways of running our lives.

This pair is a little different in that it actually refers back to choices or preferences you have already thought about."

 On a flip chart, show an example of two whole types (e.g. INTJ and INFJ) and demonstrate as you speak.

"If we say someone has a Judging preference, it means they use, in the outside world, their Judging function. For example, for this INTJ, having a J preference means that, in the outer world, this person likes to use the decision-making function, which in this case, is Thinking.

If you were an INFJ, you would still like to use the decision-making function in the outside world, but in that case it would be Feeling because your decision-making preference is Feeling.

Note that the person with a preference for Judging would rather get on with making the decision, while the person with a preference for Perceiving would really rather just take in the information and not worry about the decision.

If we say someone has a Perceiving preference, it means they use, in the outside world, their Perceiving function. For example, for an INTP, having a P preference means that, in the outer world, this person likes to use the information-gathering function, which in this case, is Intuition. If you prefer ISTP, you would still like to use the information-gathering function in the outside world, but in that case it would be Sensing because your information-gathering preference is Sensing.

The important thing is that the person with a preference for Perceiving would rather focus on gathering information and perhaps put off making a decision, while the person with a preference for Judging would rather get on with making the decision, not worrying about getting more information.

Let's look at these preferences in more detail."

Review the Judging and Perceiving preferences, using V-9A through V-9G.

Keep in mind any negative adjectives used to describe the students in the skit and mention how they are also positives.

Refer to V-9G.

"The cartoon near the bottom of the visual expresses the possibility of change. Remember that just because we have always done things one way—used one preference, it doesn't mean we can't use the other.

And once again, Judging types need Perceiving types and vice versa. Both preferences bring valuable perspectives to the table.

If you think back to our skit, you see how these preferences can have an enormous impact in our daily lives. Because Perceiving types are curious about many ideas during the process, they are hesitant to finalize the project before absolutely necessary. This can be very valuable because those who prefer Perceiving usually remain flexible, spontaneous, and open to new ideas. Those who prefer Judging can be valuable because they focus on the end product and make sure closure is reached.

A little later we will look at how some of these characteristics are seen as negative instead of valuable."

The question of procrastination often comes up at this time. If it does, say the following:

"People often assume that those who prefer Perceiving procrastinate. However, studies have shown that everyone procrastinates but for different reasons. This procrastination is often type related because different types avoid different kinds of tasks. For example, a person who prefers Feeling may avoid a task that will create tension. A person who prefers Extraversion may avoid a task that requires being alone for a long period of time."

Give examples of Judging and Perceiving from other classes and your own experience.

Use cartoons as appropriate to amplify the meaning of these preferences.

"Which of these two preferences do you think our society in general approves of most?"

The answer is usually Judging. Allow students to give different opinions and examples.

"OK, which of the two preferences are favored in this group's environment (school, youth group, etc.)?"

The answer will depend on the group but allow them to discuss and give examples.

"This bias and resulting pressure toward one preference in your environment might be causing you to use a nonpreferred approach. While any person CAN use both preferences, you feel more comfortable with one of them. If forced to use your nonpreferred over a long period of time, you can become stressed."

Step 4: Ask participants to complete worksheets. (5 minutes)

As before, have participants make their choice on the *First Guess Type* worksheet.

Have students get out the *Who Influences You?* worksheet and work on it for this pair.

"For each preference, we have reviewed who might influence you to disguise your natural preference. It is particularly important to consider influences for the J–P pair because they are so often presented as 'shoulds' or as 'issues of self-discipline or effort.' For example, an advisor or coach at school might feel that you are showing a lack of discipline by not having a consistent practice schedule. That might lead you to feel you should prefer Judging, even though you actually prefer a more flexible approach.

Or if you prefer Judging, your sister, who perhaps prefers Perceiving, may chide you for being uptight and never wanting to do anything spontaneous. In that way, she gives you the impression that it would be 'better' to prefer Perceiving."

Remember to probe to see that people understand these examples, because teens tend not to ask if they don't get something.

"Do you have some examples of influences about these preferences?"

Walk around as they work and help anyone who is having trouble.

"Which preference in this pair do you think our society values most?"

Often the group concludes that Judging was traditionally more valued, but that in this day of rapid change, Perceiving is being seen as very valuable because of its flexibility and openness to new ideas.

"We are now going to look at how your knowledge of this preference pair can be helpful in real life."

Step 5: Conduct application exercise: *The Line-Up.* (10 minutes)

Ask the participants to line up in a single line, following your instructions:

"There is a line marked with masking tape on the floor. Suppose you have a big school project due in 30 days. If you would most likely start the project on the first day, stand at the end of the line (marked '1'). If you would more likely start on the 30th day, stand at the other end of the line (marked '30'). The rest of you, please arrange yourselves along the line according to when you would start the project. In other words, those who would start about day 15 stand about in the middle. No one is recording this information, so feel comfortable being honest!"

For younger students, you might want to use a shorter period such as a week or two.

There will be laughter and bantering as students arrange themselves and compare approaches. Encourage lightness in the discussion, since you are asking them to admit some unorthodox views and radical differences.

When everyone is lined up, ask those who put J on their *First Guess Type* worksheet to raise their hands; then the Ps. Chances are, most of the Js will be on the "1" end and most of the Ps will be on the "30" end. If you have time, you can probe the reasons for any exceptions.

Now have the line bend into a horseshoe so that the "1"s and the "30"s are facing one another. This will naturally form pairs with one person from the "1" end and one person from the "30" end. If necessary, you can also have trios.

"In these pairs or trios, I would like you to do the following:
- *Each person will have one minute to talk.*
- *During your minute, you should say the following:*
  - ‣ *what words you would like to hear used to describe your work style,*
  - ‣ *what words you would not like to hear used to describe your work style."*

Give a reminder when the first minute is up so everyone gets a chance.

"What did you learn about people who use the opposite preference, that is, who work in a very different way from you?"

Facilitate a discussion about this question.

"What are some positive words you would use to describe a person who works in the opposite way from you?"

Facilitate a discussion about this question.

"Note that you were asked to share positives first. This is because we tend to see both preferences viewed negatively at times. People who prefer Judging can be labeled as compulsive and judgmental; those who prefer Perceiving as undependable and disorganized. But, as we saw in the skit, and in some of the examples that were given, both preferences have value; the key is to recognize the value of each.

In school and other environments, you will often work with people of the opposite preference, and you will need to be aware of how your preference affects them and vice versa. It is easy to see some of the problems these differences might create. How can we use our under-standing to avoid those problems?

What are some things each of us can do to work successfully with someone of the opposite preference on a project?"

Keep the focus on adaptations rather than on describing the problems.

"Finally—the time has come. We are going to look at the results of your Indicators and compare them to your First Guess Type work-sheet. Then we will see if we can come up with the type that fits you best."

Have everyone return to their seats.

UNIT 6
What's Your Type

Total Time: 15 minutes

Step 1: Introduce type dynamics and the concept of captain and first mate. (2 minutes)

Step 2: Introduce the best-fit process. (2 minutes)

Step 3: Individual exercise: best-fit type. (10 minutes)

Step 4: Summarize the best-fit process. (1 minute)

Step 1: Introduce type dynamics and captain and first mate.

"You are now going to look at what type you think you may be. Best-fit type is the one you believe at this time fits you best. It might be the one you put on your First Guess Type worksheet. It might be the one from the Indicator. It might be a combination of those two.

Up to now you have focused on the pairs of preferences. Now we are going to put them together to find a whole type."

Write any four letter type on a flip chart and use it to illustrate the following:

"There are two important things to understand about what happens when you put the preferences together.

1. A Myers-Briggs Type Indicator personality type is made up of four letters, one from each pair of preferences. But your type is not just the results of the characteristics of one preference added to another to another and so on. Each preference interacts with the others in what is called a 'dynamic' way.

For example, a person who prefers Introversion is different— if he or she also prefers Thinking—from a person who prefers Introversion and Feeling. You might even say that he or she introverts differently when Feeling is the preference rather than Thinking. Because of these interactions, or dynamics, I will be asking you to read descriptions of whole types as you start working to determine your best-fit type.

2. Because of the interaction of the preferences, each four-letter type has what we will call a captain. This is one of the two center preferences. The captain tends to be the preference that overrides the others when necessary, the one that determines a person's first reaction to a situation."

Show V-10, *Captain and First Mate*, and use it to illustrate the following:

On a flip chart, write INTP.

"Here is one example: the captain for an INTP is Thinking. This person's first and perhaps strongest reaction to a decision or information is to their Thinking preference: to look for the logic or the rules to follow in a situation. The second strongest preference, or the next one to come into play, will be the other center letter, in this case Intuition. This second preference can be thought of as the first mate of the ship.

So the captain is often in charge and wants to do things their way. But the captain often needs the first mate pulling on their sleeve, saying, 'Wait, there are some other things going on here. You need to use both preferences.'

There is a formula for figuring out the captain and first mate for each type. But for our purpose, we will tell you the captain for each type when we give you the type descriptions."

Write on a flip chart these two types: ENTJ and ENFJ.

"Sometimes, looking at the captains of several types will help you to recognize the best fit for you. For example, a person considering ENTJ and ENFJ will look at the captains of those two types (T for ENTJ and F for ENFJ). Because this person is consistently concerned with the effect of events on people, the captain is more likely F and ENFJ is more likely the best-fit type."

(Add more examples of this kind if needed.)

"Many people get concerned at this point that they are being put in boxes. But when you think about it, we are doing that more when we make assumptions about someone because of their job, or their clothes, or their appearance. Here are some ways to show you how type is different from being put in box or labeled:

- *Only you can decide which type you are. No one else can 'put' you in a type box.*

- *Type is determined by preferences you have, not by external factors.*

- *You are free to rethink your type and decide you have different preferences than you first chose."*

Show V-11, *16-Room House*.

"Sometimes it helps to think of type more as a large house with many rooms. As a person, you will feel comfortable in certain rooms and less comfortable in others. There will probably be one room that is your favorite—it has your things, maybe the posters you like, a good view, comfortable furniture, your music. You can also go to other rooms and enjoy being there. But when in doubt, you go to your favorite. Type is the same way. It doesn't confine you to a room. It just helps you find the one that seems most comfortable for you."

Step 2: Introduce the best-fit process. (2 minutes)

Show V-12, *Finding the Type that Fits You Best!* (which is also in the participant packets that you will soon distribute).

"In a few minutes you will receive a sheet that looks like this. On the second set of spaces, your results from the Indicator will be written. Please remember, this is not like a school test: The Indicator results are not necessarily right. ONLY YOU will decide which type fits you best!

You will enter the results from your First Guess Type worksheet and compare the two. Sometimes they will be the same. Sometimes they will not.

Then you will have a chance to explore why the two might be different and decide which one seems to fit you best."

Show V-13, *Why MBTI® Results and First Guess Type May Differ.*

"There are a number of reasons why the Indicator results and your own first guess might be different. Here are a few of them."

Walk through the reasons but do not belabor the points. Emphasize throughout this unit that the Indicator is not necessarily right.

Show V-12 again and write on the overhead (or use a prepared visual for an LCD projector) INFJ for first guess and ENFJ for the MBTI result.

"Let's look at how somebody might arrive at their best-fit type. Let's look at Maria who had a first guess of INFJ but ENFJ for Indicator results.

There is only one preference difference between those two types. But the two types are very different. Maria's first step would be to read the descriptions of the two types: INFJ and ENFJ. She would recognize herself clearly in one of these two and the best fit is found.

If still undecided, Maria might consider the following:

- *Social bias might have led her to choose Extraversion answers on the Indicator. It just seemed a better thing to be.*

- *Her friends might have influenced her because her friends seem to prefer Extraversion. They're always telling her she should do this or get involved with that.*

- *Which middle letter seems more like her captain, that is, the type preference she most easily identifies with?*

Maria finally decides on INFJ by looking at her captain. If she were ENFJ, her captain would be Feeling. But she observes that N is really her default, her first reaction. She generally goes first to the possibilities of a situation."

Spending time on this and other examples adds greatly to the value participants gain from the *best-fit type* exercise that follows.

Step 3: Individual exercise: best-fit type. (10 minutes)

"For this next period, about 10 minutes, you will need to work alone, to concentrate on your own results without discussing them with others. You'll have plenty of time later to share your results. However, remember everyone has a choice about when and how much they share."

Write on a flip chart **WHADJA**.

"I want you each to WAIT for someone to offer rather than saying: WHADJA—as in Whadja get on E-I? Whadja type come out?"

Pass out the Feedback Packets personally to each participant, being careful to match the correct name with the person.

"Take a few minutes to compare your first guess with your MBTI result, look at the **Who Influences You?** *worksheet and think about what you REALLY prefer. Remember that this is a puzzling out process, not a formula. It's OK not to have a final answer. I am available to help you work through differences or answer questions if you wish."*

If necessary, you can structure this time by asking the participants to do Step 1, then announcing when they should go on to Steps 2 and 3.

It is essential to maintain a quiet serious atmosphere while people are still reading. Speak individually to students who start to converse or move around, and encourage them instead to look at some of the books about teens and type that you have provided. Adhering to quiet time honors Introversion and Sensing preferences.

It is essential at this time that the facilitator is available to help students who need it. If someone looks confused, approach them, since teens seldom ask for help. Speak one-on-one in a low voice. Do not get into a long conversation with any one participant. Remember that you are there to help them ask the right questions, not to TELL them what their type is.

After 5 to 10 minutes, allow students to interact if they wish to. This will probably happen naturally, but try to maintain some quiet time first.

 When it looks as though most people are finished, show *Type Table Frequencies* (V-14). At this point in the program, participants often ask about how type is distributed in the general population.

Ask for reactions or questions about the best-fit process.

Encourage people to talk to you after class if they still have questions about which type fits them best. If you feel comfortable, give people your e-mail or telephone number to contact you with further questions.

4

Step 4: Summarize the best-fit process. (1 minute)

"This is an important process, thinking about what you REALLY prefer. I want you to remember four points about your MBTI personality type:

1. *Only you can determine your type. The Indicator is not automatically right. No one knows your type as well as you do—not the facilitator, your peers, your parents—because you know what you PREFER, regardless of how you may act.*

2. *All types have value. If you leave this class thinking you are a good type or a bad type, the right type or the wrong type, I will not have done my job.*

3. *You may not know your type right away. It may not be clear for a week or a month or longer. You may want to work with your best-fit hypothesis but continue to reflect, to talk with others, and even to read more about type, until you feel comfortable with the type with which you have identified.*

4. *Type is not an excuse. Personality type is a tool to manage yourself, to understand what makes you tick, and to understand others. In some cases, you will need to use preferences that are not yours in order to meet expectations and move towards your goals. Knowledge of type will help you anticipate tasks or circumstances that are difficult for you, but it will not remove those tasks.*

Now that you have a better idea of your own type, we are going to spend the last part of the program giving you some ideas about how type can help you in your everyday life. You will be amazed at how many ways you can use it."

Call a break of 10 minutes and be sure it goes no longer than 15 minutes.

 Always stay in the room during the breaks and make yourself available for students to approach you with questions or concerns.

-- 15 MINUTE BREAK --

UNIT 7
Type in Real Life
Total Time: 50 minutes

Step 1: E–I application exercise: *Managing Your Energy.* *(20 minutes)*

Step 1: T–F application exercise: *Can I Use the Car?* *(20 minutes)*

Step 3: What Has Been Learned. *(5 minutes)*

Step 4: Review: "Now That You Know About Type." *(2 minutes)*

Step 5: Read the monologue: "What Might Happen Next Tuesday." *(2 minutes)*

Step 6: Thanks and evaluations. *(1 minute)*

Step 1: E–I application exercise: *Managing Your Energy.* (20 mins)

"Information about type—especially your own type—is only useful if it helps you understand yourself and other people in your normal life. We have already looked at how knowledge of Sensing and Intuition might help you in writing essays and test questions. We have looked at the impact of Judging and Perceiving on how you plan and work on projects. Now, during this last part of the program, we are going to take a look at using your knowledge of Extraversion and Introversion and your knowledge of Thinking and Feeling. Interestingly enough both of these applications involve parents.

Let's start with dividing into E and I groups, based on your best-fit type at this time. For any group of more than 6 people, please form a second group."

Distribute *Managing Your Energy* (PM-3), and have participants read it.

"Sometimes, circumstances or other people require you to go against your preference, and so you need to find a way to deal with this situation. This exercise is practice in doing just that. As we do this exercise consider what you need based on your type preference."

Review quickly how the exercise will work. Give each group flip chart paper for notes.

"Are there any questions?"

Allow 10 minutes for groups to work.

When time is up, ask each group to briefly share their ideas.

Results will vary from group to group.

"OK, so we can see that there are going to be times when Introverts have to use their Extraversion, even when they don't really want to, and vice versa. But you can make things a lot better for yourself by trying some of these ideas:

- *Think about how to recognize what energizes you and what does not.*

- *Realize it is OK to defend doing what energizes you.*

- *Find ways to compensate when you are required to spend time in your nonpreferred world at a time you would rather be in your preferred.*

And thanks to your presentations, we have seen some very specific and creative ways to do that."

I didn't realize that people could be so different. Now I can understand why some people think and act in ways that I don't. It's interesting.

Step 2: T–F application exercise: *Can I Use the Car?* (20 minutes)

"The next exercise looks at how you might use your knowledge of Thinking and Feeling preferences in your own lives, in that tricky area of getting someone else to agree to something.

Please divide yourself into groups based on your best-fit preference, T or F. If any group has more than 6 people, please divide into two groups."

(If using this exercise with younger teens, change the scenario to having permission to go somewhere in a car with a friend's older brother or sister.)

Read and/or visually display the following text:

> *You have been given permission to use the family car to pick up some friends and drive to a party. At the last minute you discover the party has been moved to another friend's house who lives further away. Your parents (or the head of your household) change their minds and say you can't use the car. How do you persuade them to let you use the car?*
> —adapted from *Type Talk* by Otto Kroeger and Janet Thuesen

"Your assignment is to decide exactly what you would say to convince the person who gave you permission originally to let you use the car. You will for this part of the exercise surmise that the person has your same preference (T or F). In other words, the T group will present their argument in a way appropriate for T parents. The F group will assume they are presenting to F parents.

Choose one group member to actually speak to the class as though the parents were present.

Remember: We do not want a strategy or summary. We want to hear the exact words you would use to appeal to someone with preferences like yours."

Allow about 5 minutes for the groups to work. Check to be sure each group understands the assignment and has chosen a speaker.

Ask the chosen speaker for each group to present the words they would say to the parents.

If a group gives only a general approach, insist they provide the actual words.

After each group speaks, ask the following question in relation to each preference:

"Do the rest of you think this argument would appeal to the parents of this preference? What might you add? What do you think they wouldn't like?"

If groups don't notice things, share your own observations and examples from the words that appealed to each preference, T and F.

"From this exercise, you can see that when you want to convince someone, you need to appeal to the person's natural mode of deciding. If the person's preference is not the same as yours, think about what will appeal to their preference. You might even get help from someone of their preference before trying to make the case.

What are some other situations in your lives where it might be important to understand a person's preferred way of making decisions?

Remember that often you won't know a person's preference. Or there may be several people to convince. So, when trying to convince someone, it is often best to use points that will appeal to both preferences."

Step 3: What Has Been Learned. (5 minutes)

"We've talked about a lot of things today and you have done some thinking about your type and the types of some other people in your world. Let's just take a minute to consider the major message that you are taking away from this day."

Allow a minute for people to formulate some ideas.

Have a flip chart ready to record responses.

Some responses from programs we have presented:

> ▸ *Don't judge others.*

> ▸ *One type is not better than another.*

> ▸ *Don't force people to share their types.*

> ▸ *Your type can be influenced by your environment.*

> ▸ *You are born with one preference from each pair but you can use both ways and try new things.*

> ▸ *You can change yourself but not others.*

> ▸ *You can guess but you'll never know someone else's type for certain.*

> ▸ *Don't tell people their type.*

> ▸ *Don't share another person's type without permission.*

At the end, wait a minute to be sure those with a preference for Introversion have had a chance to think and decide if they want to speak.

Step 4: Review "Now That You Know About Type." (2 minutes)

Review "Now That You Know About Type" in a light way. Avoid being too "preachy."

Step 5: Read the monologue: "What Might Happen Next Tuesday."

"You won't remember everything we have said today. But whether or not you remember the details, chances are some of the ideas will be lurking in the form of a little voice in your brain. Here's what might happen next Tuesday."

Read the monologue below entitled "What Might Happen Next Tuesday," giving it a dramatic tone but without overdoing it. No discussion or explanation is needed.

Monologue: "What Might Happen Next Tuesday"

Will type make a difference in your life? Well, maybe, maybe not. Let's take a look into the future, say next Tuesday.

You walk in the door. There is your mother (or whoever is in charge of the household).

> *How was school today?*

> *Do you have a lot of homework?*

> *Did you ever find your jacket?*

> *Chris called. Better call him back before it gets too late.*

You start to say:

> *Leave me alone. I can run my own life.*

But wait . . .

An inner voice in your brain says:

> *Hey stupid, maybe this is just about differences.*

You respond to the inner voice:

> *Naaaaah. She's different all right she's a pain!*

And the voice responds:

(Voice) *MAYBE she's just one of those types that likes everything settled.*

(You) *But it is settled! I'm on top of it.*

(Voice) *But she doesn't know that.*

(You) *Oh. Yeah. OK. Maybe I'll give her a break.*

So you say . . .

Mom, I've got a lot on my mind here. But I know you worry about everything getting done and going the way you plan. Yes, I'm on the jacket problem and the homework. I already talked to Chris. Thanks, see you later.

Your mother looks stunned and says:

OK honey. There's some casserole in the oven if you're hungry.

Step 6: Thanks and evaluations. (1 minute)

Conclude the session by thanking everyone for their participation.

Ask the participants to complete whatever evaluation forms you normally use. Distribute the forms and explain that their comments are important for improving future sessions. Ask participants to leave the completed forms face down on their desks or tables. They do not need to sign their evaluations.

Being a teen has been really hard for me--learning how to relate to my parents and my teachers, and my schoolmates. Learning about type is helping me to figure how to better handle those relationships.

PART THREE

extras

5

options and additional materials

5

options and additional materials

Options and Adaptations

Timing

Discovering Type with Teens requires 4 hours, including two short breaks. A pre-program session is also needed to explain and administer the Myers-Briggs Type Indicator instrument.

The program can be delivered in one session. It can also be delivered in several shorter sessions. Breaking up the program has some advantages:

- ◗ Shorter sessions are easier to schedule.
- ◗ The time between sessions allows for reinforcement and digestion of the lessons.

A single session also has some advantages:

- ◗ There is less likelihood of "losing" participants.
- ◗ There is no need to build momentum each time.
- ◗ There are fewer transportation and logistical hassles.

If you decide to break the program into shorter sessions, you can combine the administration of the instrument with the introductory unit or even the first two units.

Another option is to administer the questionnaire in one session, then schedule the other units in the time frame you have. We would caution you that in our experience it is best not to split up units six and seven. If you have scheduled more than one session, do not split any individual units.

Presenting Type to Teens *Without* Using the Indicator

We have found that the interest level and impact of a type program is sharply reduced when teens do not take the MBTI instrument and receive feedback on the results. Teens in particular love to learn about themselves and this is a powerful motivator. Sometimes a student wants simply to receive the feedback without attending the program. This absolutely should not be done.

Having said that, there are some circumstances in which the Indicator must be left out of the program or the program can not be presented at all. There might be several reasons for this:

- The cost of the instrument (although the MBTI questionnaire is very reasonable compared to other instruments).
- The difficulty of obtaining permission from parents or local authorities. (This can often, but not always, be overcome by careful explanation of the program and the instrument.)
- The time involved in administering and scoring large numbers of instruments.
- The lack of a certified individual to purchase and score the instruments.

Even after a long day at school I look forward to a social activity-- it energizes me. My parents have a hard time understanding that.

If you have no alternative but to introduce personality type without using the questionnaire, then we suggest the following steps:

Step 1: Present the program in the normal way, using the visual illustrations and descriptions. A few of the fishbowl exercises require groups based on Indicator results. These can be replaced by some of the exercises described in "Alternate Exercises" beginning on page 154.

Step 2: Ask teens to self-select each preference in the way presented in the program.

Step 3: Based on their self-selection only (since no Indicator results are available), have full type descriptions available for participants to review.

You will, of course, have to delete the references to the Indicator in your presentation. You can still use the feedback packet, simply explaining why the Indicator results lines are blank.

Use of the Myers-Briggs Type Indicator Instrument and this Program

Our experience is based on the Myers-Briggs Type Indicator instrument, a widely used assessment with more than fifty years of use and numerous studies and volumes of collected data attesting to its reliability and validity. We do not recommend using another personality instrument, whether from a book, a web site, or a pencil-and-paper self-report, especially with this program, which has been designed to be used with the MBTI instrument. Other personality assessment instruments do not have the same history of reliability and validity.

Since young people live in a test-driven world, they tend to believe any "test results." So giving them feedback based on an unproven instrument is a disservice.

If the MBTI instrument cannot be used for some reason, it is better for participants to rely on their own interpretation of the preferences as they are presented for determination of their first-guess type.

Using Type Tables in the Program

We have not included the use of type tables as a normal part of this program. However, they can be used in several ways if appropriate to the needs of your group and to your own level of knowledge.

- You can share the type table for the group, which you made up as part of your preparation. This shows how the group works together or communicates. If you are going to do this, we suggest the following steps:

Step 1: During the program, keep a type table on the wall for reference.

Step 2: Introduce a type table and explain how to read it. If possible use type tables that use symbols rather than percentages, making them easier to read.

Step 3: Show a sample type table and ask what can be learned about the group from studying it.

Step 4: Show a blank type table and suggest that, when they are ready, each person who has verified a type should put an x in the box for that type. Names are not necessary; simply have each person put an x in the appropriate box.

Step 5: Show the resulting type table and discuss the implications for the group it represents:

- ▶ What may the group be good at?

- ▶ What may the group do less well?

- ▶ Who might be listened to most in the group? Least?

- ▶ Who should be listened to, because they may present a missing view?

If the group is intact and ongoing, you can even summarize by having the group decide on action to minimize the weaknesses of their type mix and take advantages of its strengths.

- Type tables can also be used to show how differences in types between two groups provide perspective about how those groups best communicate or work together. If you choose to address this point, the following two pairs of type tables (RM-6 and RM-7, RM-8 and RM-9) can help illustrate your point:

  - ▶ Suppose the counselors working with runaway youth (RM-6) had to present program ideas to the local police force (RM-7): Could there be communication problems?

  - ▶ If the fine artists (RM-8) were preparing to ask the corporate managers (RM-9) for funding: Would they have to adjust the way they make their requests?

  - ▶ Type tables can also be used to show how certain types are more frequent in certain careers. In that case, be sure to point out that these tables show only what types choose that career, not whether they are happy with that work or good at what they do.

(For additional type tables, contact the Center for Applications of Psychological Type, www.capt.org.)

fyi

Teens who are nearing graduation tend to be interested in the career choice type tables. They may entreat you to pause longer on certain type tables or ask for type tables about fields in which they are interested. Often there is not time to go into a lot of detail and you cannot reasonably be prepared with all the possible type tables and careers choices to cover all the possibilities. Be sure to tell participants that type tables show only which careers have been chosen by the various types. Type tables don't tell who is satisfied or successful in these careers or how long individuals stay in them. Type tables should not determine whether a person should try one field or not. *(Refer to chapter 12 in the* MBTI® Manual *for more information on type and careers.)*

Using This Program with At-Risk Students

This section outlines steps and suggestions for using this program with at-risk teens. If you are experienced working with this population, you may wish to make additional adaptations as needed for your specific groups.

Types of At-Risk Teens

There are many types of at-risk students and the adaptation needed will vary accordingly. So begin by defining the type of risk. Here are a few examples of risks faced by teens:

 ▶ Non-academic acculturation—simply not used to working in a formal learning environment

 ▶ Learning disability—ADHD

 ▶ Language, reading, or other learning disability

 ▶ Absenteeism

 ▶ English as a second language

 ▶ Test aversion, possibly with past failure experiences

Challenges of Working with At-Risk Students

A group of at-risk students may present one or more of these challenges:

 ▶ Restlessness, inability to sit still for long periods; need for hands-on activities

 ▶ Less responsive—don't talk as much or give as many answers to questions

 ▶ Take longer to take in new information or make links with other information

 ▶ Less retention of material

 ▶ Difficulty accepting the concept that they will determine their own type

 ▶ More evidence of the influence of others on their choices and opinions

 ▶ Resistance—often shown in body language—to being there, to your ideas, and to the idea of type

Adapting the Program for At-Risk Teens

Following are some suggested adaptations for at-risk students. Although some are true of all teens, they are more important with at-risk teens. Consider each suggestion in light of the kind of the at-risk students involved in your particular situation.

 ▶ Use more activities than with other groups; for example, create a simple guessing game to keep the students engaged. Make transparencies of the cartoons. Cut the transparencies into individual cartoons and descriptive statements removing the preference word. As you show each cartoon and statement with an overhead projector, have the students guess to which preference it belongs. Or make cartoons into a deck of cards that can be sorted by preferences.

 ▶ Use activities that allow moving around, such as matching preferences with clues on posters around the room, letting kids toss a sponge ball as they talk, or asking teens to show visuals.

 ▶ Provide snacks during activities (know special diet requirements, if any, before buying snacks).

 ▶ Use dyads or small groups with volunteer readers to read type descriptions aloud if necessary.

 ▶ Ensure that activities are not threatening and do not have right and wrong answers.

 ▶ If a teen is test adverse or frequently absent, do not administer the MBTI questionnaire.

- Review the learning frequently in games or contests.

- Relate learning to real life; for example, use case studies or ask students to apply type to an advice column for teens or to solve a teacher or parent problem. Share your own experiences of being helped by type knowledge.

- Let participants *experience* preferences rather than just talking about them; for example, building something from LEGOs, pipe cleaners and other materials, as a way to demonstrate S and N.

- If reading is a problem, consider using the Murphy-Meisgeier Type Indicator for Children® (MMTIC®)instrument, which is designed for children grades 2 through 8.

- Provide food if students are not eating at home.

- Provide sensory options during breaks using music, paper and markers, snacks, or even dancing.

- Before introducing the four-letter type code, check to see if students understand the concept of abbreviations. Give examples such as TV or CD. Also make sure that they recognize words such as psychology, theory, concept, associations, and influence.

- To capture the students' interest, tell the history of Isabel Briggs like a story.

Regardless of the kind of students to whom you are presenting, it is important to accept that every group and every individual, at-risk or not, will take away different lessons about type and will remember those ideas that are most useful to them. The facilitator serves best by not trying to drive every point home and not pressuring students to "get" everything that is said. Remember that type is only a small part of life and learning about it will not fix everything in a student's life.

Because I have strong opinions about things, my friends say I am dogmatic. But to me some things are right and others are wrong.

Additional Exercises

The two exercises below might be useful in addition to the standard program. The first is designed to allay fears about the Indicator. The second is useful as an icebreaker, especially when teens in the group do not know one another.

Not a Test

The exercise below is excellent if you have some extra time and you want to emphasize why the Myers-Briggs Type Indicator instrument is not threatening and will not be used to judge the participants.

It should be used, if at all, before administering the Indicator or during the introductory unit.

Purpose: To demonstrate that the Myers-Briggs Type Indicator is an indicator, NOT a test.

Time: 10 minutes

Materials: Paper and pencils for each participant

Process: Individual writing followed by group discussion

> **Step 1:** Ask the group to take about a minute to think, then write a list of the tests they have taken or presume they will take in their lives.

> **Step 2:** Ask the following questions, which you have also put on visual or flip chart for their reference:
> - Where did the results of the test go?
> - Who got the results of the test and made decisions based on them?
> - Were there right and wrong answers?
> - Were they allowed to change the results of the test?

> **Step 3:** Let students compare lists and experiences in pairs or trios for about two or three minutes.

> **Step 4:** Summarize with whole group. Create a list of some typical tests from the group:
> - Classroom tests: math, spelling, English, etc.
> - Standardized tests: California Achievement Tests® (CAT), Metropolitan Achievement Tests® (MAT8)

- College boards: SAT® and other achievement tests

- State tests for high school graduation

- Driving tests, etc.

Step 5: Discuss the following questions with the whole group

- Were there right and wrong answers and who decided?

- How much time was taken to explain the results to you?

- How many received the results of the tests and where are the results now (in a student file or were they sent to a college, the state or military)?

- Who made decisions based on the results of these tests—self or others?

Step 6: Explain how the Myers-Briggs Type Indicator instrument is different.

- There are no right or wrong answers.

- *You* get the results, and they cannot be shared without your permission with anyone except the facilitator.

- You can verify your type, which may be different than your reported type.

- No one should make a decision about you based on the results of the MBTI results. This includes any predictions about who you will get along with or not, what you will do or won't do well, in what major or job you would succeed, where you should go to college, if you should be hired, etc.

- The results will be explained in a workshop with lots of activities and will take about four hours. And there will be food!

Icebreaker Activity

The following exercise is useful if the group members do not know each other. It should be used before beginning the program.

If you are working with teens that do not know each other or want to encourage a sense of trust, you will need to devote time to group building. This exercise has teens ask low-risk questions of one another in a very simple way to help them get to know each other as they form the workshop group.

Step 1: Review how the *People Scavenger Hunt* (RM-4) works; modify the list to fit your group.

Step 2: Give each participant a pencil and a copy of the list (RM-4).

Step 3: Allow about 15 minutes for teens to walk around asking questions of one another.

Step 4: At the end of 15 minutes re-gather the group.

Step 5: Remark positively on the enthusiasm you saw as they got to know each other.

Step 6: Ask for comments on any interesting finds or discoveries. Ask which was the hardest to find. Do not belabor this discussion; it is meant to be just fun.

Alternate Exercises

The following are alternatives to the exercises given in the standard program. In some cases they replace an exercise to demonstrate a pair of preferences before they are introduced. In other cases, there are application exercises that can be used after the preferences have been introduced and participants have made their first guess about their preferences. The suggested use of each exercise is indicated.

Alternative E–I Exercise #1 (Anne of Green Gables)

(Use before the preferences are introduced.)

> We both had experiences when our favorite exercises fell flat, maybe because group members didn't know or trust each other or for some other reason. A video clip can be a stand in. This is a solid example that can guide you as you make or choose a video. It lasts about three minutes and provides chunks of monologue that give a glimpse of cognitive functions behind behavior. You will want to use a video that fits the age and culture of your group. Be sure to preview it yourself for language and behavior.

Be certain to obtain all required approval prior to using videos in public presentations. Certain videos are protected and inquiry should be made to ensure permission has been granted.

Purpose: To introduce Extraversion–Introversion

Time: 40 to 45 minutes

Materials: Flip chart and markers; video of *Anne of Green Gables*

Process: Film and discussion

> **Step 1:** Tell the group that they are going to look at some extreme differences in people from the film, *Anne of Green Gables*. Anne is meeting Matt for the first time. Ask the group to look for differences in personality, not age or gender. Watch for body language, such as reaching out to interact; and for conversation style, such as the amount of "wait time" between spoken thoughts and the amount of talking about one's self.
>
> **Step 2:** Show the 3-minute clip beginning with Matt picking Anne up at the train station and ending with them riding off in the carriage with their backs to the audience.
>
> **Step 3:** Ask the participants what they saw.
>
> **Step 4:** On a flip chart, make two columns entitled ANNE and MATT. Write people's observations under each one. If you get adjectives such as "shy," "doesn't say much," "polite," "friendly," "talks too much," or "rude," write them down but be sure to add descriptions such as "waits for a break to speak up," "puts out lots of ideas, one after another," and other non-stereotypical descriptions.
>
> **Step 5:** Make the observation that one person is doing all the talking and that differences like this lead to some negative descriptions and lack of appreciation.
>
> **Step 6:** Point out that Anne is beginning to observe herself. She is growing up and showing self-awareness when she asks, "Am I talking too much?"
>
> **Step 7:** Ask the following: "What could Anne do to allow Matt time to talk? What could Matt do if he wanted to join in?" Point out that they can change how they act while not changing who they are.

Step 8: Point out how Anne is actually finding her thoughts by talking a lot.

Step 9: Re-examine the content of the discussion and point out why references to "friendly" or "shy" do not relate to these preferences.

Alternate E–I Exercise #2 (E and I Participation)
(Use after the preferences are introduced.)

Purpose: To prompt actions that support E and I after concepts have been introduced and students have selected a preference.

Time: 35 to 45 minutes

Materials: Flip chart and markers

Process: Small group discussions. Use self-selection to sort into E–I groups.

> **Step 1**: Tell the group that since they know about E–I differences, they can implement changes that will improve their communication and interaction when they are together.
>
> **Step 2**: Ask the class to divide into groups of 5 or 6 people, based on their first guess for the E and I preferences.
>
> **Step 3**: Ask each group to think about specific examples of how to ensure that people with both E and I preferences participate equally in group discussions.
>
> **Step 4**: Direct groups to be specific about what is working or not working and what they could do to expand processing time and inclusion. Focus the groups' responses on behaviors and remind them to record them. Try to get specific solutions from this exercise by giving an example of what you are looking for, such as a talking stick.
>
> **Step 5**: Ask them to recall or devise new strategies and to list them. Encourage participants to include an observation and feedback process that allows for monitoring themselves as individuals and as a group.
>
> **Step 6**: Have each group share their suggestions. Suggest they think about which of the actions might be implemented in their environment.

Alternate S–N Exercise #1 (Red Badge of Courage)

(Use after the preferences are introduced. This exercise is adapted from the work of Carolyn Mamchur.)

Purpose: To demonstrate differences between Sensing and Intuition and to give teens an opportunity to explore why they focus on different kinds of information and prefer different kinds of test questions.

Time: 45 minutes

Materials: Flip charts, markers, pencil, and paper for each participant, plus the following excerpt from *Red Badge of Courage*:

> Chapter 1, about paragraph 18. Begin with *". . . one night, as he lay in bed"* and continue to *"feeling suddenly ashamed of his purposes . . ."*

Process:

Step 1: In advance, time how long it takes you to read the excerpt.

Step 2: Tell the group they may want to write as they listen while you read a passage.

Step 3: Read the excerpt to the whole group.

Step 4: Say this to the group:

> *Write two or three questions you would like to be asked if you were going to have a test on the reading. Write the kind of questions you answer easily and would do well on.*

Step 5: Have people divide into groups of S and N, according to their first-guess type.

Step 6: Ask each group to share their individual ideas and have a reporter ready to read the list of five to seven questions. Give them about 5 minutes for discussion.

Step 7: Have each group report by reading its questions.

Step 8: Contrast and compare responses from the two groups highlighting S and N differences.

Step 9: Lead a discussion about why these questions are important to people with each preference. For example, one girl said she needed many details so she could picture the scene. She needed to know how many shirts, socks, and the kind of jam. She had to see numbers of items in color to know about their relationships. Details let her know how the mother felt about Henry.

Teachers and students alike report that they would never think to ask questions like the ones written by the opposite group.

Save the responses to use in the future, either as posters or as visuals on an overhead or LCD projector. You may get differences like the following to share with other groups.

Examples of questions favored by teachers and students with a preference for Sensing:

> *What is the boy's name?*

> *What should Henry be aware of?*

> *What was the mother doing during the speech?*

> *What got packed?*

Examples of questions favored by teachers and students with a preference for Intuition:

> *Why did Henry enlist?*

> *Will Henry listen to the mother?*

> *What is their attitude towards each other?*

> *What is the mother's impression of the army?*

Alternate S–N Exercise #2 (Broadway Bound Skit)
(Use after the preferences are introduced.)

A reproducible master of the script *Broadway Bound* (RM-5) is located on the CD-ROM that accompanies this book.

The skit has one scene with two people. Each person has two dialogue sheets printed on a piece of oak tag. The actors read the dialogue and use the props as noted.

Purpose: To illustrate that the two perceiving functions are complementary, equally valuable, and useable by all types.

Time: 35 to 45 minutes

Materials: Markers, flip chart, and dialogue sheets (RM-5) for each actor; props for the Sensing actor (magnifying glass, dictionary, map or atlas, appointment calendars) and for the Intuition actor (small light bulbs mounted on "antenna," appointment calendar).

Process: Skit followed by class discussion

Step 1: Before the program, coach the actors to "keep it light" and to keep emotions out of it. While it is okay to show some rolling of the eyes, it is important to complete the dialogue without physical signs of emotion such as clenched fist or jaw, voices raised in pitch or volume, slamming table, etc. If emotion is present, the conversation does not demonstrate type.

Also before the program, show the actors how each partner is paying attention to a particular kind of information.

Examples:
Sensing: specific information in regard to distance, name of a state, accuracy in regard to time of day and mileage, spelling, and an *initial* lack of interest in the ideas and future possibilities.

Intuition: general comments about main idea, big picture blend of ideas, *initial* lack of interest in details.

Step 2: Tell the group they are going to look at some differences in people.

Step 3: Perform the skit. (Teens enjoy seeing their teachers in these roles.)

Step 4: Facilitate a discussion about the different information each person prefers.

Questions for discussion:
- *What kind of information does each person seem to look for?*
- *What kind of information is each person not interested in?*
- *What are the strengths each person brings to the relationship?*
- *What advice can you give to each partner about communication with someone of the opposite preference?*

Options and Additional Materials

Alternate T–F Exercise #1 (Bugs in the Classroom)
(Use after the preferences are introduced.)

Purpose: To introduce differences in T–F decision making.

Time: 45 to 60 minutes

Materials: Flip chart, markers, and enough copies of the student letter and response letter from this exercise for each student and/or one copy for facilitator to read to the group.

Process: Class discussion followed by small self-selected T–F group discussions.

> **Step 1**: Read "Bugs in the Classroom" letters, samples 1 and 2 to the group (page 161).
>
> **Step 2**: Have the class identify the differences in the students' responses. Put each writer's characteristics on separate flip-chart paper.
>
> **Step 3**: Ask the class which student they think has preferences for F and which for T.
>
> **Step 4**: Ask students to sort into groups according to their first guess for T or F.
>
> **Step 5**: Have type groups describe and report the strengths that students of each preference bring to the classroom and how each strength might be demonstrated.
>
> **Step 6**: When they report, note how the T and F group attribute "strengths." Do they attribute more strengths to the letter writer who shares their preference?

 This exercise uses gender neutral names and provides opportunities to note and/or discuss male/female stereotypes.

(This exercise is based on a letter written by Kyla Alper-Ernst and published in a teacher newsletter from Antioch New England Graduate School. Used here with permission.)

Options and Additional Materials

Bugs in the Classroom (Sample 1)

Sample one is a letter from Dale, a seventh grade student. Sample two is a response to Dale from another student, Taylor.

Dear 7th Grade Science Teacher,

I am writing this letter to you because of what we have recently been doing in your science class. I am strongly against dropping bugs in alcohol, watching them suffer and drown, stabbing pins through their dead bodies, and then throwing them away a few weeks later. To me it is a pointless sacrifice of something so delicate yet so important. You could say there are so many bugs that killing a couple hundred won't hurt the population, but what if giants came to earth and killed a couple hundred people and mounted them on their walls? What if one of those giants killed your mother or father or friend or you? How would you like to be drowned in a jar of alcohol with bodies of your friends and families floating around? The idea makes me think of the Holocaust, where basically the same thing happened to people.

I can understand why a scientist would kill bugs, so that they can study them, but I can't understand why every 7th grader on our team has to kill a bunch of bugs. I think that it is sending the wrong message to the students. Science class should be about studying the bugs in their natural habitats, not about "the more bugs you have the higher your grade will be".

Thank you,

—Dale

Bugs in the Classroom (Sample 2—Response to Dale's letter)

To: 7th Grade Teacher

Some people say they are against killing things yet they kill mosquitoes with a slap. Aren't living things living things?

Besides with the bugs there is no suffering. Alcohol kills them instantly. There may be some movement but that doesn't mean pain. Plus, they probably already gave birth so have served their purpose or whatever.

The point about giants is a weak argument. There are no giants here. Animals are not like people. In fact, in some species parents actually eat their babies.

Teachers often buy bugs that are already dead and therefore don't kill them. And there are benefits to using live specimens:

- *They are better than a picture in a book*
- *Actual, in 3D*
- *Can feel the texture and movement*
- *See actual color and stuff*

Of course, there are some negatives too:

- *May take a long time to examine*
- *Can cost more*
- *Some people are against it*

If someone has a problem with it, I'd want to know if they always do—like "oh, the bunny is cute but you can kill a rat for science or kill a mosquito because it's a nuisance." If that's the case they are just getting out of doing the work. But if they're always against killing animals, then that's different. I wouldn't fail someone for their beliefs. But I wouldn't want someone to get an A on my work. I'd just say that the problem is your problem and not my problem. Just go over there while I do my work.

I think why that student thinks different from me is because he or she has been taught by others from a very early age that killing animals is wrong and actually believes that animals have feelings.

— Taylor

Options and Additional Materials

Alternate T–F Exercise #2 (You Be the Teacher)

(Use before the preferences are introduced.)

This exercise can be used in several forms: fishbowl, small group exercise, or large group discussion. Choose the one that fits the situation.

Purpose: To demonstrate differences in Thinking and Feeling decision-making criteria and that both functions can reach similar conclusions.

Time: 45 minutes

Materials: Scenario text, flip chart, enough markers for small groups, writing paper, pens/pencils for participants.

Process: Discussion with entire group, in small T and F groups, or in the fishbowl.

> **Step 1:** Read the scenario "You Be the Teacher" (p. 164) to the group or groups.

> **Step 2:** Ask the group:
>
> ▸ Do you flunk or pass her?
>
> ▸ How do you decide? What criteria do you use?

> **Step 3:** If you use this exercise for a **class discussion**, then point out the similarities and differences in the responses. This will prepare the ground for introducing the T and F preferences.
>
> ▸ If you have used **small groups**, give the groups time to confer and then ask them to report their conclusions.
>
> ▸ This exercise can also be done as a **fishbowl**, using groups determined by their T and F scores on the Indicator. In that case, use the same process as the fishbowl in the standard program.

This exercise can be a "stereotype buster." Try to stay with the discussion about why the initial decision on passing or flunking the student was made. Reasoning from a Thinking response will sound different than reasoning from a Feeling response. You may be able to detect that one group leans toward flunking the student because of the scoring criteria, while another determines that it would be uncomfortable to live with a lie so also flunks the student. Another may pass her because "the present shouldn't influence the future" or "the odds are she'd pass next time" versus "I really trust my belief in her as a student."

You Be the Teacher Scenario

You are a 5th grade teacher. In your class you have a student who entered more than half way through the year. Without a doubt the student is the best one you've ever had. You know that she has moved around five or six times in the last few years following a divorce and some family legal problems. Because of the move and change in custody, the principal has been unable to get the girl's past school records.

You have the feeling her life is settling down, and you believe the girl is a wonderful candidate for an enhanced learning program that begins in the 6th grade.

However, because of the lack of past records, she needs to take a placement test to determine her readiness for the program. You are very strict on a cutoff of 70 percent for someone to enter the program, and you have never made an exception.

You are confident that she can earn this 70 percent minimum. In fact, you expect her to get a much higher score, based on her work in your class.

The day of the test arrives and the girl enters quietly and says she's ready. When she's done and she leaves, you review her results, you are totally shocked to see a test score of 66 percent. As you sit in silence two people who are passing your doorway are discussing the rumor that your student's brother has been expelled, after being involved in a drug incident in which another teenager died. You must hand in your enhanced learning placement list in an hour. You are the only one making the decision; you are the only one who will know her score.

▸ *What will you do?*

▸ *What factors will you make your decision on?*

(This exercise is adapted from the work of Carolyn Mamchur.)

Options and Additional Materials

Alternate J–P Exercise #1 (Planning Exercise)
(Use before the preferences are introduced.)

Purpose: To introduce J–P attitudes

Time: 25 to 30 minutes

Materials: Flip chart and markers

Process: Fishbowl; use MBTI results to select two groups: one with Judging preferences and one with Perceiving preferences.

> **Step 1:** Present people who have been chosen for the fishbowl. Ask them to leave the room.

> **Step 2:** Tell observers their job is to look at differences in how people in the fishbowl groups approach planning, how many options they look at, and how long discussions last before decisions are made. Ask them to observe these things and not to interact with the fishbowl groups.

> **Step 3:** Bring in those with J preferences first. Tell them they are part of a drama club that has just finished its fall play. They have been asked to plan a thank-you supper for the play's director and adult sponsors. It is to be held in a week.

> **Step 4:** Give the group markers and flip chart to record their process.

> **Step 5:** Tell them they will have 7 minutes to complete the plan and that you will give a 5-minute warning.

> **Step 6:** Give a 5-minute warning and stop their work after 7 minutes. Thank them and have them return to their seats.

> **Step 7:** Repeat process with the fishbowl group with P preferences.

> **Step 8:** Facilitate a discussion about similarities and differences in how the two groups approach the topic.

Those with a Judging preference often come to a decision quickly and then spend time defending and explaining it. They often approach the task with seriousness and use words like "definitely." They may emphasize with quick gestures such as pointing fingers or shaking heads in agreement or disagreement. The Judging group's flip charts may be completed in lines, with bullets. The list may be concise and short.

Those with a Perceiving preference are often having fun while they are outside the room. You may hear laughter. When they enter and sit they may tend to look "relaxed," often slouching back in chairs, hands in pockets, etc. Someone may be missing (in the bathroom, making a phone call, taking care of another task). They may begin in a round about manner, maybe talking about other things or making jokes about the task. They may take longer to begin discussing the topic (especially if they prefer Introversion as well as Perceiving). They may discuss many aspects of the topic, or question the assignment. They may not begin to make conclusions until the warning is given. The Perceiving group members may write all over the paper making additions as they come up.

Alternate J–P Exercise #2 (Change Now?)

(Use before the preferences are introduced.)

Purpose: To introduce J–P attitudes

Time: 25 to 30 minutes

Materials: Flip chart and markers

Process: Fishbowl; use MBTI results to select one group of those who prefer Judging and one group of those who prefer Perceiving.

> **Step 1:** Before the exercise begins, choose one of the following prompts for discussion:
>
> ▸ Should the teacher be allowed to change an assignment after students have begun working on it?
>
> ▸ What would you say about a teacher who extends the due date on the day the paper is due?
>
> **Step 2:** Select the people who have been chosen for the fishbowl, and ask them to leave the room.
>
> **Step 3:** Tell observers their job is to look at differences in how the fishbowl groups approach planning, how many options they look at and how long discussions last before decisions are made. Ask them to observe these things and not to interact with the fishbowl groups.
>
> **Step 4:** Bring those with J preferences in first. Tell them the topic and that they will have 5 minutes to come to a conclusion.

Step 5: Give the group markers and flip chart to record their process.

Step 6: Give a 2-minute warning and stop their discussion after 5 minutes. Thank them and have them return to their seats.

Step 7: Repeat the process with the fishbowl group with P preferences.

Step 8: Facilitate a discussion about similarities and differences in how the two fishbowl groups approached the process.

Those with a Judging preference often have definite opinions. They may feel that the change is unfair and rewards those who do not do things on time. They may take a stand quickly, and then spend time defending and explaining it. They often approach the task with seriousness and use words like "definitely." They may emphasize with quick gestures of hands or fingers, shaking heads in agreement or in disagreement. The flip charts may be completed in lines with bullets. The list may be concise and short.

Those with a Perceiving preference often see changes as no big deal, shrugging their shoulders or making dismissive gestures. They may comment that things will work out no matter what the instructor does. They may be surprised that some are upset about the change. They are more likely to make jokes and look relaxed during the discussion. Some people may not even address the issue or be missing (in the bathroom, making a phone call, taking care of another task). The group members may begin in a relaxed manner, maybe talking about other things, and may not have a serious "tone" about the task. The group may look at many points of view and perhaps change the topic. They may not even reach a conclusion. They may write all over the paper making additions as they come up during the presentation.

resources & bibliography

6

list and script for
reproducible materials

6

visuals and reproducible materials

Please note that the following list of visuals and reproducible materials are stored on the CD-ROM located on the inside back cover of this book. Each item is individually saved in a print-friendly, .pdf format. These materials are copyrighted and may not be sold or used in any other context except the administration and delivery of an MBTI presentation.

Visuals for Presentation

Reproducible Participant Materials

Reproducible Masters

Suggested Scripts for Explaining Visuals

V-6A

This character prefers Extraversion and he is actually filling his energy tank by hanging out in the world. He would lose energy if he had to spend too much time alone.

While this character down here is getting her energy from spending time alone. She would be drained of energy by too much time out in the world.

Of course, people with a preference for Introversion like to be active and hang out too, but between times they need to re-energize with some time alone.

V-6B

When a person who prefers Extraversion has something to say, he or she is more likely to say it right away—you usually know what they are thinking. While the person below, preferring Introversion, is more likely to share thoughts one-on-one with someone he or she knows pretty well.

V-6C

When people react to ideas, those who prefer Extraversion need to talk it out right away, like this person in class. No hesitation. While the person below wants to think through an idea or response before he or she is ready to speak up.

Unfortunately, this sometimes means people who prefer Introversion are left out of a discussion because by the time they have thought an idea through, the discussion is over.

V-6D

People with E and I preferences learn VERY differently. The person at the top just jumps in and acts, not stopping to think it through—learning through experience. They are often called "impulsive" as kids.

The person who prefers Introversion, on the other hand, tends to think an idea through, and THEN act, even though the family may say, "join in, go ahead, you miss out if you hesitate."

V-6E

When it comes to studying, those who prefer Extraversion will be found working together, maybe sharing a project, all talking at once—you can sometimes recognize their preference because they are so noisy!

If you prefer Introversion, you may find the group work tiring and confusing, much preferring to go off alone to do your work.

V-6F

These two E preference people are drawn to each other like magnets, wanting constantly to talk and get more energy by interacting. They often get told to "quiet down."

People with I preference have a whole universe inside their head, a universe just as interesting as the outer world. They may be oblivious to class, until the teacher pulls them back to the present by calling their name.

V-7A

Here the S preference person holds a bone and sees just what is there—it is white and triangular, with jagged edges. That's it.

But the N preference person takes the basic bone and their mind takes off—imagining it's part of a huge dinosaur skeleton—it "might be" a dinosaur.

V-7B

Both preferences are creative but in very different ways. The person preferring Sensing invents and discovers step by step, using what is known to find a new planet or build a better human being.

For the person who prefers Intuition, creativity is leaping to a totally different idea like this person who has created a being completely different being, not even close to human.

V-7C

When it comes to projects, the person who prefers Sensing will start a project with the details—getting the supplies, measuring—and then see what emerges.

But the person preferring Intuition needs to start with the big picture, where the project will end up. They might picture themselves in the finished room. Only then can they break it down into details like paint and ladders.

V-7D

S and N are about what information seems important to you. Studying WW II, the first student sees the statue and immediately thinks about the facts relating to it: who, when, exactly what happened.

The other person, with an N preference, leaps right to the bigger meaning like patriotism, the morality of war, or the cost of defense.

V-7E

When the person with a Sensing preference wants to do the best work, he or she will follow the directions for making the TV and go step by step.

But people with an Intuitive preference feel limited by directions and want to do the best work by doing the assignment in their own ways, making their own version of a TV.

V-7F

An S preference who is learning something new wants to practice and practice, like this person learning to ride a bike. They will do the same with subjects in school: keep practicing until they get it.

The N preference, on the other hand, is quickly bored with doing the same things and moves on to something different. They do the same in school, always looking for new ways to learn or do things.

V-8A

Let's look at two people choosing something, maybe a skate board. The Thinking preference person at the top might analyze all the information impersonally: quality reports, cost comparison, ease of repair. The Feeling preference person below will probably look at more personal factors: what design is appealing, brands that lots of people have, or what a friend thinks or has.

V-8B

Differences in the way people react to things can cause some real hard feelings. The first reaction of the top person, with a preference for Thinking, is to critique, to see how the statue could be better. She may praise the parts she likes, but not right away.

But the first instinct of the person below is to appreciate—to point out the things he likes about the statue. He may eventually criticize but not till much later.

V-8C

People with different preferences interpret fairness very differently. A person with a Thinking preference wants above all to be consistent: "If you are late, you are late." But a person who prefers Feeling will look at the situation, the people, the circumstances and possibly conclude: "Oh this is your first time late, so I won't count it."

V-8D

You can see the T preference is impressed—the important thing is that a teacher is competent. For a person with a Feeling preference, a good teacher is not enough—there has to be a personal connection, a real liking for the teacher.

V-8E

This Thinking person is determined to master something—here the pogo stick— and being competent is VERY important, even if it takes all night. The Feeling person seems to be putting in a lot of effort because it involves friends.

V-8F

Everyone likes recognition. But a Thinking person wants it for achievements— building the best snowman—while a Feeling person wants recognition to come from caring, from doing what he or she believes in, like working with the homeless.

V-9A

People who prefer Judging want to know what's coming up—see the map of the trail. Perceiving people, on the other hand, really get a kick out of just seeing what is going to happen. Start down the slope and come what may.

V-9B

How did the fisherman end up out in the storm? For this J preference, the plan was to go fishing and he was determined to carry out the plan, and so didn't listen to new weather reports!

The P preference also got into trouble because he wanted to be spontaneous. He took his time looking at the options and by the time he had decided, the option he chose was gone.

V-9C

For a J preference, the energy for a project is around getting started early and working regularly to avoid the anxiety of rushing near the deadline. The P preference likes to keep the project open to new ideas, then get energized by the due date.

V-9D

The Judging preference focuses on getting the work done and then knocking off to play. The Perceiving preference likes to mix the two, working a little, and then taking a few shots at the basket.

V-9E

The J and P preferences see commitments very differently. This J preference promised to finish cleaning the garage this morning and that's it. For the P preference, saying he would clean the garage was really a general intention, easily amended if circumstances change, like a friend wanting to play tennis. The plan changes and he'll finish the garage later.

V-9F

These two people start out to learn about spiders. The J preference takes a methodical approach, examining samples, studying the poster. The P preference prefers to follow his curiosity and see what he finds. He'll learn from whatever happens.

7

resources

7

resources

Submitting MBTI® Instrument Research Data

Reporting type tables is the easiest of all ways to contribute to MBTI research. We earnestly invite you to share what you have discovered. If we use your samples in their entirety, you will be credited for the type table when it appears in research data compiled by CAPT. If your data is not reported separately but is included in a composite type table with other samples, a master copy of your submitted data will be on file in the Isabel Briggs Myers Memorial Library.

Please send CAPT your tables so that we may all improve our applications of the MBTI instrument. If you have questions, write or call us and ask for the Research Services Department 352.375.0160.

How to Contribute to the CAPT Research Database

CAPT requests a clear and detailed description of the composition of your sample. There are two important reasons for this description. First, the samples in the database are an attempt to get a picture of the larger population from which they were drawn. When demographic characteristics are reported, one can determine more clearly whether the sample is an appropriate model of the larger population. Second, the samples may be composited. In order for a composite to be useful in applications and research, it is necessary to know the component parts. Vague descriptions make it risky or inappropriate to combine samples: A poorly described sample is often only marginally useful.

Here is an illustration of how poorly described data may create problems: A contributed type table of 100 teachers without any other description. Variables such as gender, age, race, subject taught, or grade level taught could influence the frequency distribution of the types, so such information is a necessary part of data collection.

And here is an example of how commingling samples results in unusable data: A type table with 67 practicing female architects, in practice for more than 5 years, between the ages of 30 and 50; and 7 secretaries. Since there is no way to determine which people in the group were secretaries and which were architects, the data is confounded and virtually unusable.

The following guidelines can minimize such problems:

1) Report samples as distinct groups; do not mix "apples and oranges." If in doubt, report data on separate sheets (it is easy for CAPT to merge them).

2) Describe the subject thoroughly.

    a) Be clear about the description of the group. Define role, occupation, or other defining characteristics in clear, definite terms.

    b) Describe how respondents were selected. Be specific about sampling methods. Was it a random sample or volunteers? State the percentage of the larger population represented by your sample (if known).

    c) Include the major demographic characteristics: age, gender, race, education level, geographic location, and any other identifying characteristics.

    d) If you wish to report a sample but maintain confidentiality, use a global generic description. For example, the Space Needle Power and Light Company in Seattle can be described as "an urban public utility company in the northwestern United States."

3) Who owns the data? List the names of all people who participated in collecting the data and the institution they represented at the time of collecting that data. If the authors should be listed as anonymous to protect confidentiality, please state so.

Your contributions to the CAPT MBTI database help in the continued growth and exploration of psychological type and its applications.

Center for Applications of Psychological Type
2815 NW 13th Street, Suite 401, Gainesville, FL 32609
800.777.2278 • 352.375.0160 • www.capt.org

Ethical Guidelines for Using the MBTI® Instrument

General

- Identify type theory as the work of C. G. Jung and the MBTI instrument as the work of Isabel Briggs Myers and Katharine C. Briggs.

- Present psychological type as **describing healthy personality differences**, not psychological disorders or fixed traits.

- Be adamant that **all types are valuable**; no type is better, healthier, or more desirable in any way.

- Describe preference and types in **nonjudgmental terms** at all times; be aware of how your own type biases may influence your words.

- Present type preferences as **tendencies, preferences, or inclinations**, rather than absolutes.

- Stress that type **does not imply excellence, competence, or natural ability**, only what is *preferred*.

- Never imply that all people of a certain type behave in the same way; type should **not be used to put people in rigid categories.**

- Explain how people **sometimes act in ways contrary to their preferences** because of pressure from family, relationships, job environment, or culture. Consistent forced use of nonpreferred preferences can cause stress.

- When describing preferences, **distinguish between what has been shown by research and what are anecdotes to illustrate type.**

Administration

- Tell respondents that taking the Indicator is **always voluntary** and offer the opportunity to not participate.

- Insist that Indicator results **never be used to label**, evaluate, or limit the respondent in any way.

- Ensure that type results are **confidential** and not given to anyone besides the respondent without permission.

- Inform respondents of the **purpose of taking** the instrument and how results will be used.

- Tell respondents the Indicator is **not a test**, since there are no right or wrong answers.

- If the instrument is given for research purposes, **sharing the results** with respondents is not required but highly recommended.

- **Do not take specific questions** from the Indicator to get a "quick reading" on a particular preference pair.

- Administer and score the Indicator in **accordance with the guidelines** in the most current edition of the *MBTI® Manual*.

Feedback

- **Give results directly to the respondent** as part of an active discussion with a certified administrator. Never deliver results in impersonal ways such as through e-mail or mail.

- Present type results as a **working hypothesis**, a starting point for further exploration.

- Make it clear that **the respondent is the expert;** the only person who can verify which type fits best.

- Allow respondents to **self-assess their preferences** based on the introduction to type, prior to giving results of the Indicator.

- Do not become defensive if the respondent disagrees with the report results. **Help the respondent explore his or her hesitations** and identify a comfortable best-fit type.

- **Provide descriptions of all sixteen types** to help determine best-fit type. Recommend additional materials for further study.

- Do not counsel a person towards or away from a particular career, relationship, or activity based solely upon type information; **type does not explain everything.**

- Make it clear that the preference clarity indexes in the results do not imply excellence, competence, or maturity. They **reflect only consistency in choosing** one preference over another.

- Make sure the respondent sees the **feedback session as the beginning of the process.** Knowing one's type is not a one-time understanding, but a guide to ongoing growth and development toward an individual's potential.

Professional Qualifications

- Even those who are certified to purchase the Indicator by their education will want to study materials specifically about the MBTI instrument so they can offer comprehensive background and guidance to a respondent. The MBTI instrument is different from other instruments. Without in-depth understanding, the feedback could be shallow or inaccurate. Perhaps most importantly, certified users who do not seek additional training may miss opportunities to use the full richness of the theory.

- Many certified users update their knowledge and expertise regularly with continuing education activities such as conferences and workshops.

Legal Guidelines

- The MBTI instrument may not be reproduced without written permission from the publisher. The trademark designation must appear on all references to the MBTI® instrument or Myers-Briggs Type Indicator® instrument. The phrase *MBTI®* (or Myers-Briggs Type Indicator®) should be used *only* as an adjective (e.g., MBTI® instrument, MBTI® tool, MBTI® results, etc.).

An exception is made for text in books, booklets, or electronic materials where there is a copyright page (or legal notices section) that contains the following statement:

> *Myers-Briggs Type Indicator, Myers-Briggs, and MBTI are trademarks or registered trademarks of the MBTI Trust, Inc. in the United States and other countries.*

In these instances, it is advised to use the trademark symbol on the first reference in each chapter (hardcopy) or page (electronic) to notify users of the ownership of the mark.

—from the Myers & Briggs Foundation Web site (www.myersbriggs.org). Used with permission.

Resources for Learning More about Type

Association for Psychological Type International (APTi)

9650 Rockville Pike
Bethesda, MD 20814-3998
301.634.7190
www.aptinternational.org

Membership organization for people who work with the MBTI instrument. Publishes the APTi Bulletin which often contains examples of how type is used.

Buros Institute of Mental Measurements

University of Nebraska-Lincoln
21 Teachers College Hall
Lincoln, NE 68588-0348
402.472.6207
www.unl.edu/buros

The Center for Applications of Psychological Type (CAPT)

2815 NW 13th Street, Suite 401
Gainesville, FL 32609
800.777.2278
www.capt.org

Not-for-profit organization that provides MBTI-related certification and advanced training programs, publishes Myers-Briggs related materials and books, and offers other personality-related instruments and training. CAPT provides an extensive online bibliography and is the site of the Isabel Briggs Myers Memorial Library.

The Myers & Briggs Foundation

2815 NW 13th Street, Suite 401
Gainesville, FL 32609
800.777.2278
www.myersbriggs.org

A not-for-profit foundation established by the Isabel Briggs family.

Consulting Psychologists Press, Inc. (CPP)

1055 Joaquin Road, 2nd Floor

Mountain View, CA 94043

800.624-1765

www.cpp.com

Publisher of the Myers-Briggs Type Indicator instrument and of MBTI-related books and materials.

www.TypeCan.com

A Web site created for and by teens that introduces type in an upbeat, creative, and inspiring way. Interactive graphics and videos makes this Web site a hit with young people of all ages.

The Type Reporter

11314 Chapel Road

Fairfax Station, VA 22039

703.764.5370

www.typereporter.com

A periodic newsletter with articles about personality type.

Bibliography

Alcock, M. W. and P. Ryan (2000). "ADD, type and teaching." *Journal of Psychological Type*, 52:5–10.

Block, J. R. (2002). *Seeing double*. NY: Routledge.

Crane, S. (1964). *The red badge of courage*. NY: Bantam Books.

DiTiberio, J. and A. Hammer (1993). *Introduction to type in college*. Palo Alto, CA: Consulting Psychologist Press, Inc.

Fairhurst, A. M. and L. M. Fairhurst (1995*). Effective teaching, effective learning: making the personality connection in your classroom*. Palo Alto, CA: Davies-Black Publishing.

Fields, M. and J. Reid (1999). *Shape up your program! tips, teasers & thoughts for type trainers*. Gainesville, FL: Center for Applications of Psychological Type, Inc.

Gilligan, C. (1993). *In a different voice: Psychological type theory and women's development*. Cambridge, MA: Harvard University Press.

Ginn, C. (1995). *Families: Using type to enhance mutual understanding*. Gainesville, FL: Center for Applications of Psychological Type, Inc.

Golden, B. (1994*). Self-esteem and psychological type: definitions, interactions, and expressions*. Gainesville, FL: Center for Applications of Psychological Type, Inc.

Golden, B. (2001*). Portraits of self-esteem: Sixteen paths to competency and self worth*. Gainesville, FL: Center for Applications of Psychological Type, Inc.

Jensen, G. (1987). *Learning styles*. In J. Provost and S. Anchors, *Applications of the Myers-Briggs Type Indicator in higher education*. Palo Alto, CA: Consulting Psychologist Press, Inc., *(pp. 181–206)*.

Kroeger, O. and Thuesen, J. (1988). *Type talk*. NY: Dell Publishing.

Lawrence, G. (2009). *People types and tiger stripes* (4th edition). Gainesville, FL: Center for Applications of Psychological Type, Inc.

Lawrence, G. (1997). *Looking at type and learning styles*. Gainesville, FL: Center for Applications of Psychological Type, Inc.

Lawrence, G. D. (2004). *The zig-zag model for problem solving*. Gainesville, FL: Center for Applications of Psychological Type, Inc.

Martin, C. (1995). *Looking at type and careers*. Gainesville, FL: Center for Applications of Psychological Type, Inc.

Meisgeier, C. and E. Murphy (1987). *Murphy-Meisgeier Type Indicator for Children: manual*. Palo Alto, CA: Consulting Psychologist Press, Inc.

Meisgeier, C., E. Murphy, and C. Meisgeier (1989). *A teachers guide to type*. Gainesville, FL: Center for Applications of Psychological Type, Inc.

Myers, I. and P. Myers (1980). *Gifts differing*. Palo Alto, CA: Consulting Psychologist Press, Inc.

Myers, I., L. Kirby, and K. Myers (1998). *Introduction to type* (6th edition). Palo Alto, CA: Consulting Psychologist Press, Inc.

Myers, I., M. McCaulley, N. Quenk, and A. Hammer (1998). *MBTI manual: A guide to the development and use of the Myers-Briggs Type Indicator* (3rd Edition). Palo Alto, CA: Consulting Psychologist Press, Inc.

Murphy, E. (1992). *The developing child: Using Jungian type to understand children.* Palo Alto, CA: Consulting Psychologist Press, Inc.

Pearman, R. (2002). *Introduction to type and emotional intelligence.* Palo Alto, CA: Consulting Psychologists Press, Inc.

Provost, J. (1993). *Applications of the Myers-Briggs Type Indicator in counseling: a casebook.* Gainesville, FL: Center for Applications of Psychological Type, Inc.

Provost, J. (1988). *Procrastination: Using psychological type concepts to help students.* Gainesville, FL: Center for Applications of Psychological Type, Inc.

Provost, J. (1993) *Strategies for success: Using type to do better in high school and college.* Gainesville, FL: Center for Applications of Psychological Type, Inc.

Saunders, F. W. (1991). *Katharine and Isabel: Mother's light, daughter's journey.* Palo Alto, CA: Consulting Psychologists Press, Inc.

Scanlon, S. (1992, November–1993, May) "Kid types." *Type Reporter,* 47–50.

Scanlon, S. (2000, February) "Your ideal education." *Type Reporter, (*76)1–8.

Scanlon, S. (1990, June) "Writing your natural way." *Type Reporter,* (5)1.

Stice, J. E., ed. *Developing critical thinking and problem solving abilities.* San Francisco, CA: Jossey-Bass.

The Authors

Mollie Allen, M.Ed, is a certified coach and teacher who works with individuals and groups. She has undergraduate degrees in Child Development and Education and a M.Ed. in Administration and Supervision. She uses typology and the *Myers Briggs Type Indicator*® (MBTI®) instrument because these tools provide positive models of human development and help adults and children understand the mystery of personality differences.

For 15 years she designed and facilitated workshops that introduced typology and the MBTI instrument to high school seniors studying humanities. Her master's research and much of the material in *Discovering Type with Teens* is based on her field work with hundreds of students. Mollie has written articles for the newsletter published by the Association for Psychological Type International and presented at APTi conferences. For many years she was active in the Boston and New Hampshire chapters and Northeast Region of APTi.

Mollie applies type, the MBTI instrument, and the coaching model with adults and students who are investigating life changes, college selection, career exploration, and organization and study skills. She helps students of all ages with reading, accent reduction, spelling and writing difficulties. She also works with groups of supervisors, managers, and volunteers in a variety of settings. Mollie is an MBTI® Master Practitioner and member of APTi, and the Learning Disabilities Association. She is the mother of four children.

Claire Hayman has been involved with the MBTI instrument since she was qualified in 1990, and since then she has attended numerous related conferences and advanced trainings. She has applied MBTI theory both professionally and personally to facilitate personal growth and enhance relationships. She administered and interpreted the MBTI instrument annually for the tenth graders at Snowden International School in Boston where she was the Student Support Coordinator and Guidance Counselor from 1997 to 2007. Previously, she consulted with numerous individuals and organizations as an MBTI practitioner.

Claire was active in the Association for Psychological Type as president of the Boston Chapter (BACAPT) from 1992 to 1996 for which she earned the APTi Chapter Leader Award. As a result of the strength of BACAPT, Boston was chosen for the APTi Conference in 1997. She then served as the Northeast Regional Chair, from 1996 to 1998. Claire has also been an APTi workshop presenter. She has taught social studies in both public and private schools, and has raised a son and daughter.

Kay Abella is a qualified administrator of the *Myers-Briggs Type Indicator* instrument and has presented type programs nationally and internationally to business and nonprofit organizations and in churches, schools, and social service settings. Educated at the University of California at Berkeley, she worked as a journalist and an organizational consultant. Eventually, she decided to focus on psychological type because she felt it was the most effective tool she had ever used to help people understand and change their behavior. She was co-founder and co-editor of TypeWorks, a professional newsletter for people using the MBTI instrument in organizations. Her books include *Building Effective Training Programs* (Addison-Wesley, 1986) and *Fighting Castro: A Love Story* (Wingspan Press, 2007).

Resources

Getting Better Results by Appreciating Differences:
Introducing Psychological Type to Schools

*This well organized and easy-to-use guide for educators
covers all important aspects for implementing psychological type
in learning environments . . . from improving team collaboration
with faculty to improving individual student achievement.*

*The accompanying CD-ROM has over 200 pages of
reproducible resources for teachers, including sample lesson plans
that address the differing learning needs of students.*

PUBLISHED BY THE CENTER FOR APPLICATIONS OF PSYCHOLOGICAL TYPE, INC.
VISIT WWW.CAPT.ORG OR CALL 800-777-2278.

every child appreciated. every child engaged.®

The Murphy-Meisgeier Type indicator for Children® (MMTIC®) assessment was developed specifically to measure psychological type in young people. Used with elementary, middle, and high school students the MMTIC assessment comes with age-specific type reports that address each child's strengths and challenges in school, as well as how they might respond in close relationships.

An easy-to-use online interface facilitates administration for the teacher, educational consultant, or adult who is responsible for the administration of the assessment. Comprehensive support materials are available for all levels, including a career report for middle and high school students. The MMTIC interface is available through www.capt.org.

MURPHY-MEISGEIER **type indicator for children**®

Published by the Center for Applications of Psychological Type, Inc. ⋅ www.capt.org ⋅ 800-777-2278

The fourth edition of Gordon Lawrence's "gold standard" of books about psychological type.

Offers ideas and insight for improving student achievement by using psychological type in schools.

Includes exercises, charts, tables, and a primer for introducing type effectively into organizations.

PUBLISHED BY THE CENTER FOR APPLICATIONS OF PSYCHOLOGICAL TYPE, INC.
VISIT WWW.CAPT.ORG OR CALL 800-777-2278.

The MMTIC® Training Program

Teaching educators how to use type in schools.

For teachers, counselors, administrators—this
two-day training program is for anyone who wants to use
psychological type to help students reach their
full potential using the Murphy-MeisgeierType Indicator
for Children® (MMTIC®) instrument.

MURPHY-MEISGEIER **type indicator for children**®

Presented by the Center for Applications of Psychological Type, Inc. Visit www.capt.org or call 800-777-2278.

The MBTI® Certification Program

Get certified to purchase and administer the MBTI instrument from the company co-founded by Isabel Myers.

The Myers-Briggs Type Indicator® instrument is
the most widely used personality assessment in the world.
Becoming certified allows you to successfully use
psychological type to improve achievement for everyone
in the education process.

Presented by the Center for Applications of Psychological Type, Inc. Visit www.capt.org or call 800-777-2278.

(This program is presented with the approval of CPP, Inc., ("CPP"), the publisher of the Myers-Briggs Type Indicator instrument.)